Writing
for Radio

WRITING HANDBOOKS

Also available from the series

Writing for Radio

CHRISTOPHER WILLIAM HILL

Bloomsbury Academic
An imprint of Bloomsbury Publishing Plc

B L O O M S B U R Y
LONDON • NEW DELHI • NEW YORK • SYDNEY

Bloomsbury Academic
An imprint of Bloomsbury Publishing Plc

50 Bedford Square	1385 Broadway
London	New York
WC1B 3DP	NY 10018
UK	USA

www.bloomsbury.com

BLOOMSBURY and the Diana logo are trademarks of Bloomsbury Publishing Plc

First published 2015

© Christopher William Hill, 2015

British Library Cataloguing-in-Publication Data
A catalogue record for this book is available from the British Library.

ISBN: PB: 978-1-4081-3983-7
       ePDF: 978-1-4081-4389-6
       ePub: 978-1-4081-4388-9

Library of Congress Cataloging-in-Publication Data
A catalog record for this book is available from the Library of Congress.

Typeset by Fakenham Prepress Solutions, Fakenham, Norfolk NR21 8NN
Printed and bound in India

Radio is CGI for the soul.
JOHNNY VEGAS

Writing for Radio

Why Radio Anyway?

Are you a regular listener to the radio? Imagine that you switch on the radio and you hear the following:

MAGGIE: And that was the moment I decided to move to the isolated Scottish island where I met Ted, the taciturn stranger and shell-collector. Our lives collided and I knew that nothing would ever be the same again …

I call this the 'Scottish Island of Impending Tragedy' school of writing. There's a lot of it out there. Recently I tuned into BBC Radio Four, part way through the Afternoon Drama. A character had died, the funeral was being discussed. My heart sank. It's easy to form the impression that a radio play is not quite a radio play unless the central character succumbs to illness and dies. Writers spend a lot of time on their own so it's little wonder that they often have a morbid preoccupation with death. Of course, I'm not suggesting for one minute that this subject matter should be off-limits, but variety really is the spice of life. And that's the problem. A lot of radio writers, especially writers at an early stage in their careers, sit down to write the sort of radio play they *think* they should be writing, rather than the sort of radio play that they might actually enjoy listening to.

What Makes Radio Special?

I'll be honest with you; it took me a while to appreciate what makes radio unique, without constantly wishing it was a different dramatic medium altogether. So if you're coming to radio with some suspicions about the form and a nagging doubt that it's an outdated and limiting type of drama – I understand. I understand, but at the same type I hope I can change your mind.

So let's start bravely:

FORGET EVERYTHING YOU THOUGHT YOU EVER KNEW ABOUT RADIO DRAMA!

In theatre, writers often talk about the 'fourth wall' – that invisible peephole into the lives of the characters on stage. In radio it's rather a different sensation – the listener is inviting the characters into the home. It's not like switching on the television where drama is safely locked away behind the screen. On the radio, characters exist in the ether – they breathe the same air as the listener. This immediacy is one of the real joys of the medium.

Theatre Versus Radio

A man goes to the theatre. The play begins and, for reasons unknown, the man instantly takes against the play – but politeness or embarrassment prevents him walking out. No matter how miserable he feels and how ill-disposed towards the cast and playwright, he will probably sit through the first act, planning his escape from the theatre as soon as he reaches the interval. And who knows, by the time the interval comes round, things may have looked up. Our theatregoer has suddenly become absorbed in the play. He's curious to find out what happens next, so he settles down in his seat and decides to stay until the end.

Unfortunately, this is rarely the case with radio. Although some listeners may be content to let a boring play continue as background noise, a serious listener will probably reach over and – CLICK – the play is no more. Alas, the hand of the listener is rarely far away from the on/off switch and it's never a bad idea to remind writers of that grim fact at the earliest possible moment.

So how do we prevent the listener cutting the play off in mid-flow? The answer is a simple one:

KEEP YOUR AUDIENCE INTERESTED AND KEEP THEM ENTERTAINED

See, I told you it was simple!

Not Quite a Captive Audience

The BBC is still the world leader in terms of radio drama output and offers much scope, both for the established dramatist and the novice. For most first-time radio writers the first port of call will be the Afternoon Drama, a 45-minute daily slot on BBC Radio 4, each script running to approximately 7,500 words including all dialogue and sound effects directions (of which more later). Much of this book is geared towards the afternoon broadcast slot, although the majority of my suggestions are equally applicable to all other available slots.

Periodically the BBC conducts surveys to determine exactly how listeners occupy themselves as they're listening to the radio. Sometimes, it seems, the listener may actually leave the house mid-way through the play. That's right – depressing as this may sound, it is a reality. For some listeners the Afternoon Drama For some listeners the Afternoon Drama unfortunately coincides with the school run and any number of other daytime chores.

So what am I suggesting you do with this information? Well, nothing really. Push it to the farthermost reaches of your mind. But remember – you are competing for the listener's attention, so give them more reasons to tune in than switch off!

But there is an important point to make here – and the point is this; it is your responsibility to distract the listener to such an extent that he or she leaves the iron merrily smoking away on the ironing board and forgets to pick up the children from school. And radio has the power to achieve all this and more.

> DO EVERYTHING YOU CAN TO DRAW THE LISTENER
> INTO THE PLAY

I'm not suggesting for one minute that a radio play should be a frivolous affair – it can be whatever you want it to be. But don't disregard the needs of your listener. After all, the essential function of a radio play is to entertain on some level.

There is No System

A lot of advice in this book is based on workshops I have led, talking to writers new to radio. On the face of it, radio drama can seem like a peculiarly technical medium, and in some respects it is just that. But don't be put off – after you've mastered a few basic requirements, it's no more complex than any other dramatic form.

There is no foolproof formula to writing a good radio play. I've learned a lot by trial and error.

Inside the Radio Studio

We're all familiar with those clichéd radio effects from the halcyon days of radio production – the sound of doors being slammed and bolted, hard-soled shoes tapping on polished wooden surfaces, the clatter of coconut shells to simulate horseshoes, etc. It might surprise you to discover just how technologically advanced a modern radio studio is – a Pandora's Box of gadgets and gizmos. So let's take a tour around a radio drama studio. Rest assured, you won't need a working knowledge of any of this equipment, but I think it's useful to know what you have at your disposal.

The View from the Cubicle

Before we enter the studio itself, we'll quickly visit the cubicle – the nerve centre for any radio production. The cubicle is broken up into four main sections:

1 At the far end of the room a large mix desk is used by the Studio Manager (SM) to record a radio play. As far as I'm concerned, the less a writer knows about this expensive bit of kit the better.

2 Alongside the mix desk is desk space that's used by the Production Coordinator (PC) during recording. The PC (rather like a stage manager in the theatre) is responsible for keeping the production on track – checking the running time of each scene, listening out for line errors and taking note of each separate take and which version has ultimately been 'bought' by the producer.

3 In the centre of the room a long table is occupied by the producer and the writer – with a talkback

microphone to communicate with the actors in the studio.

4 In a corner of the cubicle a computer screen is set aside for a second SM (GRAMS) who will select and add in pre-recorded sound effects during recording.

A large window above the SM's desk looks out over the main studio space beyond the cubicle. More often than not, the actors will be visible through this window. However, if the actors are recording in the farther-flung corners of the studio they will be picked up on a video monitor above the studio manager's head allowing the producer and the SM to keep track of the cast.

Now, into the studio!

Dead Room

A dead room is far less sinister than it may sound. Fans of *The Archers* will have heard countless scenes recorded in such a space. Imagine that you're standing in the middle of a deserted and grassy field. You see a friend 50 yards away and you shout out to get their attention. What happens to your voice? If you have no idea, then I encourage you to find a field and experiment. The simple answer is this – there's no echo in a field. The voice becomes absorbed into the landscape. To replicate this effect, the dead room is generally made up of carpeted or foam-covered walls to rob the actors' voices of an echo. Exterior sound effects will then be mixed in to build up the picture – birdsong, a distant aeroplane, a whispering breeze, etc.

Stairs

There will always be a flight of stairs in the studio, often connecting the main studio space to a practical upper gallery. The staircase will usually have three different surface textures: concrete, wood and carpet – useful for creating both exterior and interior effects. Imagine a character escaping down a tower block stairwell, climbing the wooden staircase of a stately home, or running down the stairs of a terraced house to collect the post. Hearing an actor running off mic or onto mic can add a sense of movement to a scene and will create a greater sense of authenticity than simply walking on the spot.

Sound Trap

A sound trap is a sharply tapering passageway, often rounding a sharp corner and ending in a small chamber. It is another way of producing the effect of characters walking off mic – or standing at a great distance. Imagine you're recording a dramatisation of *Casablanca* and Rick and Captain Renault are walking off to begin their beautiful friendship – a sound trap could add authenticity to this iconic scene.

Windows

High up in a wall, a small sash window looks out over the studio. Perfect for the balcony scene of *Romeo and Juliet*, perhaps, or an eighteenth-century Londoner emptying out her chamber pot on the street below.

Like Home-From-Home

It's not unusual to find a purpose-built kitchen space in one corner of the studio, with a sink and running water, microwave and all mod cons. Some studios are even equipped with a small bedroom space, including bed – occasionally actors will be found asleep there between scenes.

Screens

Screens, often moved into position on castors, can be used to create confined spaces in the studio – telephone boxes, car interiors, etc.

Spot Effects Area

Spot effects are those sounds which are produced live in the studio – for example, the unmistakable crackle of the turning pages of a newspaper or the distinctive crunch of footsteps on a gravel path.

In some corner of the studio you will find a shelf unit, stacked with a peculiar assortment of odds and ends that can be used to produce a wide range of sound effects. Grass, for example, is often replicated by walking through piles of unspooled audiotape. There are also bundles of clothes – invaluable when you want to create the sound of a character dressing or undressing.

Spot Effects are frequently layered with recorded sound effects to build up a sound picture. I once wrote a yapping Pekinese dog into a script – he played a pivotal role in the drama and it was important to make the creature as realistic as possible. The dog was essentially a ball of fluff on the end of a stick, attached to which was a small bell – this was operated live in the studio by an SM. The yapping was a pre-recorded track that was added in separately. It was this layering of effects that created the authentic-sounding animal. It was this layering of effects that created the authentic-sounding animal.

And with that, our whistle-stop trip around the radio studio is at an end. We'll close the door for now but as you set to work on your play always remember that in the studio, with a little imagination, anything is possible.

How to Lay Out a Radio Script

The BBC has never supplied me with a pre-approved template for laying out a radio script. Personally, I always take against radio scripts that are formatted to look like screenplays – I can't help but get the feeling that the dramatist would much rather write for the movies.

There's nothing that you can't format on your own so long as you have a working knowledge of how to tabulate text and write in upper case. The most important thing is to make the text clear and easily readable.

The most important thing is to make the text clear and easily readable. So let's begin at the beginning. It's always useful to start each scene with an uppercase heading:

SCENE ONE: INT. BOOKSHOP. DAY.

Or alternatively:

SCENE ONE: EXT. STREET. NIGHT.

INT and EXT indicate whether the scene is an interior or an exterior, a helpful little nudge for the studio manager who will be responsible for bringing the scene to life. In the interior of a bookshop we may well hear the buzz of electric lights, or the bleep of a barcode scanner. The exterior street setting would probably suggest the rumble of passing traffic, the bustle of pedestrians walking along a pavement, etc. It's not necessary for you to add this level of detail – the heading says enough. Of course, if it's important to clarify something out of the ordinary you can do so at the top of the scene in the following way, with F/X indicating sound effects (note that the F/X notes are also in uppercase and underlined):

F/X: THE SHOP IS CROWDED FOR THE BOOK SIGNING.

Or:

F/X: THE STREET IS EERILY QUIET. A LONE CAR ROARS PAST.

The indentation of scene headings and F/X notes helps to make the script more easily readable. This indentation also applies to the dialogue:

ANGELA: Is the kettle on, Steve?

STEVE: Just making a pot of tea now.

Again, for ease of readability, character names are in uppercase, while dialogue is in lowercase.

    F/X notes are not simply used to add detail at the top of a scene; they also help to add authenticity throughout a scene. For example:

SCENE ONE: INT. KITCHEN. DAY.

F/X: THE KETTLE BOILS.

ANGELA:	(OFF) Steve…is the kettle on?
F/X:	<u>STEVE FILLS TEAPOT.</u>
STEVE:	Just making a pot of tea now.
F/X:	<u>STEVE TAKES MUGS FROM CUPBOARD.</u>
ANGELA:	Two sugars please!
STEVE:	You're sweet enough, Angela.

Angela's line (OFF) tells us that the character is in another room. Imagining that a microphone in a radio play works rather like a camera in a TV drama, it is clear that the listener is with Steve in the kitchen.

One helpful little note I've always cherished is (D) to suggest distortion to the voice. For example, if Steve is talking to Angela on the telephone:

F/X:	<u>STEVE TALKS ON HIS MOBILE AS KETTLE BOILS.</u>
STEVE:	Where are you?
ANGELA:	(D) Nearly home. Get the kettle on.
F/X:	<u>STEVE FILLS TEAPOT.</u>
STEVE:	It's like you've got some sort of sixth sense.
ANGELA:	Eh?
STEVE:	I'm just filling the pot.

ANGELA: Great. Any macaroons left?

If you have ever seen a production-ready radio script you might have noticed that each line of dialogue is given a number:

SCENE ONE: INT. KITCHEN. DAY.

F/X: THE KETTLE BOILS.

1. ANGELA: (ENTERING) Well, where's my tea then? I'm dead on my feet. You won't believe the day I had at work.

2. STEVE: Here you go.

F/X: STEVE PUTS MUG ON THE TABLE.

3. ANGELA: You're a star, Steve.

The numbering of lines is helpful if only a section of the scene is being recorded, or if there is a line fluff and a retake is called for. It allows the producer or studio manager to precisely pinpoint which line or lines are to be recorded: 'We'll record line 2' rather than 'We'll record the line 'Well, where's my tea then? I'm dead on my feet. You won't believe the day I had at work.'

It's useful for a writer to include page numbers but you may be delighted to learn that the numbering of lines will be added in by the Production Coordinator shortly before the recording of the play.

It's sensible to start each new scene on a clean page. This is particularly useful in studio, when the script is often taken apart so the actors need never hold more pages in their hands than is strictly necessary (thus helping to prevent the problem of noisy and disruptive

script rustle). Helpfully, many actors are now using iPads
or Android devices to download their scripts.

These days I think double line spacing looks a bit
silly on the page (and wastes paper); single line spacing
always looks too cramped. I tend to split the difference
and plump for 1.5 line spacing, which still gives the
writer, producer, production coordinator and actors
room to scribble over their script without going blind
struggling to read their own handwriting.

The Naming of Parts

Names convey much about character. I'm inclined to
think that on radio a name means even more than in
film, TV or theatre – in the absence of a clear, visual
impression of a character, the name becomes the coat
hanger on which the listener can drape a personality.

So, what does a Dorothy look like? Or a Fraser
… or a Milly? It's important for a writer to consider
what a name indicates about the age, ethnicity and
social status of a character – though it can often be
interesting to play with a listener's preconceptions too.

Allow the Listener to 'See' Your Characters

In theatre, film or television, a character who remains
silent throughout a scene can still be an important
dramatic figure. Not so on radio. The less a character
speaks the more quickly they can seem to disappear
from a scene. It's rather like spinning plates – making
sure that each character earns his or her place in the
scene.

On radio there's a limit to how much information
the listener can process without visual stimulus. It can
be hard enough keeping two characters in our head

at one time – imagine how much more difficult it becomes if you've written ten characters into the script.

If our play is set in a girls' public school, circa 1950, how can we possibly differentiate between Clara, Suzy, Mags, Lucy and Daphne? Well, I'll be honest, it's very difficult to do this, without succumbing to the temptation of supplying every character with a different accent to help the listener distinguish one from another. It's a tried and tested approach and one that you must earnestly endeavour to avoid.

Voices, like names, can suggest much about a character; sex, age, regional accent and (perhaps contentiously) class and ethnic background. I would even say, to an extent, it's possible to guess at the height and size of a character.

Painting a Scene with Sound

It should probably go without saying, but all your directions will be concerned with *sound*. If your character is wearing jogging trousers and a T-shirt, we probably wouldn't be able to hear this. In the same way the sound of casual shoes on a pavement would make no discernible noise – whereas we *would* be able to pick up the distinctive click of more formal footwear.

So here's another example of a sound effect that would probably fail to add anything to a scene:

F/X: SHE CLOSES HER EYES.

This could be a powerful moment in a film, but conveys nothing at all on radio.

What Sort of Person Are You?

Most characters are abstractions of our own selves. In fact, it's sometimes difficult to tell exactly where a writer ends and a character begins.

Drawing on your own personal experiences can help imbue your writing with the authentic ring of truth. We take the raw subject matter of life and convert it into drama.

A Moment of Self-Analysis

Okay then, let's get down to brass tacks. For reasons that should become apparent, I firmly believe that we need to understand something of our *own* character before we can begin to create fictional characters. So, what sort of character are you?

Think of those awkward silences when you meet someone for the very first time. What do you say? Are you one of those people who like to fill the silence, or would you rather keep quiet? Are you the sort of person who gives away a lot or a little?

A playwright friend of mine always tells me that I'm too open and I give away too much about myself. That's probably true. But what else do I know about me? This calls for a bit of Freudian self-analysis. Here goes …

1 I am an incurable hypochondriac.

2 I enjoy meeting new people.

3 I often pretend to understand things, rather than appear stupid by confessing, 'Actually, I have absolutely no idea what you're on about.'

4 I attempt to cover my Obsessive Compulsive Disorder by pretending to be absent-minded.

5 I worry about big things and tiny things but very little in between.

Does this provide enough information to begin constructing a character? Which personality traits might be useful to a writer? Every hero has a fatal flaw – you could call it a 'character hole' – and I always look for these 'failings' when I am writing a play.

Public and Private

It's important to consider the contrast between the public and the private face of your characters. In other words, that which we are prepared to reveal, and that which stays safely locked away inside our skulls. Radio can exploit this discrepancy – making explicit the innermost workings of a character's mind.

Rhythms of Speech

There's no such thing as a consistent character – we're constantly changing. Our rhythms of speech and choice of vocabulary depend entirely on the situations in which we find ourselves and on the people who surround us in any given moment. How do you communicate with your friends, your family, your work colleagues – how might you adjust your speech if you're talking to a disobedient child, or an elderly stranger?

Imagine that your character is in the middle of a job interview. He or she is perhaps more aware of every question they're answering. The language becomes more formal as the character makes a conscious effort to complete sentences elegantly. Our rhythms of speech are in a perpetual state of flux.

What You See is What You Get?

There's nothing worse than a 'what you see is what you get' character. Or rather, a 'what you hear is what you get' character. As in real life, characters should be complicated – neither all good, nor all bad. Prone to the human failings that trip us up on a daily basis.

I realised that for a long time I'd been writing a certain type of central character; a wide-eyed innocent who would stagger through the play waiting for other characters to explain everything to him. And this character was me. Ever since then I've battled the urge to make my protagonists 'nice'. It's such a horrible word, isn't it? It's horrible because it's lacking in dramatic potential.

Or is it?

I was talking to a first-time radio dramatist who was writing a play about Harry, a pensioner, his daughter Sarah, and Carol, Harry's carer.

The writer was struggling. I asked her what conclusions she'd reached about Carol. She was sure that the character was overweight and that she had almost certainly spent her childhood in a foster home. But this still seemed slightly external, and didn't communicate much about what made the character tick. I asked her if Carol was a 'nice person'. The writer made the point that all characters start out nice; it's what fate throws at them along the way that alters this. Again, this was fine, but it didn't explain how the character might become the catalyst for dramatic conflict in the play. So I pushed. I asked if Carol *liked* Harry.

'She doesn't have any feelings about Harry.'

I asked the writer if Carol liked Sarah. The answer was the same.

'She doesn't have any feelings for Sarah.'

This was fantastic. It became apparent that the character, a carer, had no compassion for the patients or the families she was dealing with – a carer *who didn't care*. Suddenly a whole host of dramatic possibilities presented themselves.

Toptext and Subtext

Often good dialogue can get in the way of a good plot. You can see it meandering its way across the page – it's well written, it's possibly even entertaining at times, but it lacks drive. And without drive, there's no drama. Maybe the word 'dialogue' has been misused here, so perhaps it might be worth noting the difference between conversation and dialogue. Conversation is the humdrum and everyday chatter of the 'real world'. Dialogue, however, is dramatically motivated speech – it has a purpose, a focus, a sense of direction. It is *crafted* speech and there is often a discrepancy between what characters say and what they think. This is generally referred to as TOPTEXT and SUBTEXT.

Toptext is quite simply the dialogue as written on the page. Subtext is the implied dramatic undercurrent which is not made explicit in the toptext. As a none-too-subtle example of this, let's consider the following line:

MIKE: That looks like a nice cup of tea, Graham.

So what's the subtext here? Quite possibly that Mike wants a cup of tea, and by dropping a rather obvious hint he hopes that Graham will make a cup of tea for him.

The Eavesdropping Playwright

Dramatists are magpie-like in the way they hone in on useful snippets of conversation that can be converted into dialogue. I overheard the following line recently as a woman spoke to another woman in the gym:

WOMAN: Did you have a tragic accident with your back then?

It was a wonderful moment – manna from heaven for the eavesdropping writer. But what does the toptext tell us about the woman in question – and what can we glean from the subtext? Well, who knows? If we use this random line as the basis for a created character we can assign whatever personality traits we want. So is the character clumsy in conversation? Or is she deliberately spiteful but concealing it behind a thin veneer of sympathy? Is she in some way responsible for the 'tragic accident'?

Building a Bond

Imagine that a radio play begins in the following way:

SID: I killed a man once.

It's an arresting line but this approach sets up an immediate barrier between the listener and the protagonist. Sid has condemned himself out of his own mouth. Or rather, the playwright has condemned Sid. Assuming that we believe Sid when he tells us that he killed a man (and nothing is a given here) we instantly become wary of the character – we don't want to get too close. Imagine how different it might have been if the writer allowed the listener to bond with the character – by providing reasons to like Sid. If a character is shown to be 'like us' it is obviously easier to create this empathic bond – so make the character vulnerable, make the character funny, make the character *as much like the listener as possible*. And *then* tell us that Sid has killed a man. Instantly, the listener's response becomes more complicated and undoubtedly more interesting.

Not that we always *want* to build a bond between a character and the listener. On occasions we deliberately want to keep them at arm's length. Play with your audience's expectations, don't ever pander to them.

Empowering the Listener

I've read many plays with page after page of cleverly constructed dialogue, but no underlying drama. And without drama the listener will soon be reaching for that ever-present 'off' switch. If Alice is having an affair behind Mark's back, letting the listener in on the secret can be a useful way of ratcheting up the tension. If the listener then discovers that Mark has spurned the advances of his childhood sweetheart Lily and has resigned from his job to devote himself entirely to Alice…well, you can see how the stakes keep on building.

Discovering the Hidden Bomb

In most families there's a hidden 'bomb' – that concealed piece of information that may have been locked away for years, but which will cause disaster when the fuse burns down and the information is finally revealed. Is there a bomb in your family? If so, imagine the dramatic potential if you set the fuse alight. In your head (it's best not to leave written evidence!) chart the likely fallout and the implications for the family members involved. Understanding the dramatic possibilities of our own lives can help to inform our fictional creations.

Telling Lies

Consider the ways in which we adjust stories on a daily basis. When we relate an interesting or amusing incident, we naturally think about the hook – a way of drawing the listener into our story. If we see that the story isn't being received as well as we might have hoped, we often make adjustments to pull the audience around. And then we want to draw a line under the story – to round up the action. We build the story towards an inevitable climax and tie it up with a bow.

We all make these little adjustments. We add to the story, we edit the dialogue so it's as punchy as possible and allows for a neat and satisfying conclusion. It's not a lie exactly; it's a *version* of the truth. Any re-angling or paraphrasing of the story can be forgiven in pursuit of our one goal – not to bore the listener.

The Importance of the Hook

Playwrights are always looking for the hook – providing your audience with reasons to engage with your play and to continue engaging. The writer's aim is to draw the listener in as quickly as possible. I always find it helpful to think of this in physical terms. You're baiting your hook, you're casting off (I'm told that this is what anglers do) and you're attempting to reel in the listener.

Once hooked, it is your job to prevent the listener from wriggling away.

Internal Monologues

I can completely understand why people cling to narration. But in many cases it's used lazily, to provide information that could easily be conveyed through dialogue.

An internal monologue is generally at its worst when it's simply used for 'scene shifting' – topping and tailing a scene to provide expositional detail such as time and place. Take this line for example:

MARK: I left the hotel and took a sharp left. It was a baking hot day as I crossed over the road, narrowly avoiding a cyclist and the number 48 bus …

There is a widespread misapprehension that monologues as a form are easier to pull off than dialogue. After all, it's only one person talking – what could be simpler than that?

But the sound of a single voice can have an oddly dispiriting effect on the listener. I don't enjoy being talked at, I doubt you do either. Be honest – how necessary is the narration? Do keep reminding yourself that most situations in a radio play can be dramatised through dialogue and sound effects alone.

It's One Way in My Head, it's Another Way on the Page …

Sometimes good dialogue gets lost in translation from brain to page. We can hear it in our heads but for some reason we can't quite capture it on the page.

Sometimes it's simply due to the fact that the dialogue is too complete, too formal.

For instance, how often do we really get to the end of our sentences? Rarely in life do we complete each and every thought we begin to articulate. There are many reasons for this. We might lose our thread; we could be interrupted by someone who knows instinctively where the line of conversation is going.

Punctuation can really help to break up the dialogue and give it an added sense of authenticity. For example:

I often realise, as I'm speaking, that I have absolutely no idea at all where I'm heading with … that thing that I'm trying to … you know …

(You see what I mean?)

It was a long time before I discovered that this particular punctuation mark is called:

The Ellipsis

…

It's often used to indicate that a character's thoughts are running out of steam. Or perhaps a character has reached the end of one thought and is about to go off at a conversational tangent.

The Dash

–

A dash is an indication that a character is about to be interrupted by the next line of dialogue, or even that they are about to interrupt themselves. It's different to an ellipsis, because it suggests that the character would continue with their line of thought were it not for the interruption. For example:

MAX: I suppose you think you know what you're—
SAM: Will you please stop being so patronising.

The Forward Slash

/

Caryl Churchill is a leading exponent of the forward slash, a nifty little punctuation mark that is used to produce a very specific dramatic effect:

MICK: You're serious? I asked/you not to do that, Pam.
PAM: Of course I'm serious, Mick.

It indicates to the actor playing PAM that she should jump in with her line as soon as MICK hits the forward slash – so both lines will overlap.

Actually, I'm quite a fan of the Caryl Churchill forward slash. Or rather, I'm a fan of the theory behind the Caryl Churchill forward slash, marking as it does, the crossover point where the baton of dialogue is passed from one character to the next. Some writers will use a forward slash when they actually mean to use a dash, and this makes the intention of the line unclear.

The Pause

A pause is an indeterminate period of time that can theoretically be as long as an actor or producer wishes. Of course, on the radio, we leave the listener in silence at our peril.

The Beat

A beat is a very specific break, like the tick of a metronome or a click of the fingers. Beats mean different things to different writers – but to me it's always been the split-second pause that makes a joke work. For example, why did the chicken cross the road? BEAT. To get to the other side.

Here's a chance to play around with ellipses, dashes, forward slashes, pauses and beats. This is an exercise in two parts:

The End of the Affair

Part I

You have two characters – CHARACTER A and CHARACTER B. The two characters have been in a relationship for ten years, but CHARACTER A is about to confess that he/she has been having an affair. You are allowed 15 lines of dialogue for each character and you can add in as many sound effects, or 'FX', notes as you want. Okay, pen at the ready … go!

If possible, type up this section of script and print it out. Now read the script aloud.

So, how was that? Was it easy or difficult to create the characters? Did you believe in the dialogue? Write down your feelings and keep hold of this section of script.

Part II

You're going to try that exercise again. The information is exactly the same as before. CHARACTER A is still going to confess to the affair. Again, there will be 15 lines of dialogue for each character. And as before, you can add as many sound effects as you want. But this time we're going to introduce a modification. CHARACTER A can only use three words at a time (or fewer) and CHARACTER B can only use one word. Off you go!

How did you find the exercise the second time? Was it easier or more difficult? Lay the two scripts side by side and examine the text closely. It's not always the case, but I generally find that a shorter version of a scene is more effective than a longer one. Fewer words can allow more space for the subtext to show through. Less, as they say, is often more.

What Does Your Own Home Sound Like?

I live in West London, close to the Thames. It's a very specific part of London, with its own very specific sounds. I had decided to set a play in and around my house, so I wrote out a list of familiar noises, to help establish the soundscape I wanted to create in the play:

Canada geese
Trains passing over the nearby railway bridge
Low-flying planes on landing path to Heathrow Airport
Wild parrots (believe it or not!)
The sound of Victorian sash windows rattling in the wind.

Write a list of the familiar sounds which surround you. How might they be incorporated into a radio play, in a way that provides a vivid and specific sense of place?

Where Do Your Characters Belong?

Think about how a character relates to his or her surroundings. It's worth asking why a writer decides to set a play in a chip shop rather than a pub, or a council flat rather than a suburban semi.

Sometimes the choice of location seems entirely arbitrary, and this should never be the case. The setting should contribute to the drama in some way.

Ground Plans

Long-running radio series like *The Archers* rely on ground plans to give writers and production team members a strong sense of environment. It helps them to remain consistent when recording. So if you're really struggling to picture the world of your play, why not sit down and sketch it out? If your play takes place inside one house, try drawing ground plans of each of the rooms you intend to use in your script.

Remember the Mundane

Conversations take place while we're preparing food in the kitchen, hoovering the floor in the lounge, shopping in the supermarket, driving in a car – wherever.

Make sure you know exactly where your scene is unfolding and the possible sound effects you have at your disposal to break up the dialogue and root your characters in a fully three-dimensional world. Do everything you can to hoodwink the listener into forgetting that the play was recorded with actors standing round a microphone.

Try to make sure that FX notes aren't divorced from the dialogue. For example, if we hear:

F/X: FOOTSTEPS IN CORRIDOR.

It's almost impossible to work out to whom the footsteps belong. It's a disembodied sound effect that doesn't make any visual sense.

Don't Overuse FX Notes

The majority of radio plays I read from first-time writers are awash with sound effects – and they rarely add anything. On the contrary, they often weaken the sense of the script. FX notes can quickly become a fussy 'character' in their own right, nagging away at the director and actors. Take this for example:

F/X: THE CHAIR SCRAPES ACROSS THE FLOOR.

This is an oft-used but largely redundant FX note. And here comes another FX note that always gives me the shudders:

F/X: WE HEAR HER FOOTSTEPS ON THE FLOOR.

If it's clear that the character is moving as they speak, we can confidently assume that unless they are levitating (in which case you will certainly want to make this fact explicit) then the listener *must* be able to hear footsteps. An *ipso facto* moment, if you like.

There are some writers who panic and try their hardest to pepper the script with sound effects every other line. It can become more like reading a code than a radio script and the effect is almost always bewildering. Overused FX notes can become a real barrier to understanding what the dramatist is trying to say.

Imagine you're setting a scene in a busy hospital A&E department. If it's important that an alarm is heard, or a specific doctor is called to reception, then leave it in. Otherwise, it has no business being there.

Always bear in mind that your script will be picked up by an SM who spends his or her time locked away in a recording studio, and will know instinctively how to bring your scenes to life. If you want the inside of an ocean liner, you've got it. If you want the surface of the moon, it's yours. I once heard of a studio manager searching desperately for a recording of a 1950s Cadillac. He found countless authentic sound clips, none of which convinced the producer. Finally, in desperation, he played a recording of a Sherman Tank. 'That's it,' said the producer. 'That's exactly the sound.'

To my shame, I recently wrote the following FX note:

F/X   THEY APPROACH THE GATE.

My producer could barely disguise her mirth.

Should I Always Start a Scene with F/X Notes?

No, you don't have to start a scene with FX notes although it can be a helpful way of providing clues for the listener. Be careful that the dialogue doesn't become too expositional in order to set the scene.

An Exercise in Sound

You're going to write a short scene for no more than three characters – and how you choose to do so is completely up to you. There are, however, three details that you must work into the script:

1 The scene is set in a coffee shop in London.

2 It's spring.

3 It's a cold day.

The scene should be no longer than half a page. Now write!

Did you begin your scene with the sound of Big Ben chiming? Go on, admit it, you did, didn't you? Of course, the distinctive chime of Big Ben instantly indicates London – but it's hardly subtle, is it? Let's try a less obvious approach. Think of alternative ways in which you can conjure up this setting. You can use as many sound effects as you want to help place the location. Now try the exercise again.

The Cut

The 'cut' between scenes can be a useful way of pushing the action forward. It can enable the writer to move swiftly from one scene to the next, without the necessity of crossing 'i's and dotting 't's. In short, it's a way of cutting out moments that lack dramatic drive.

It's perfectly acceptable to allow the listener to make the assumption that a piece of information has been imparted between two scenes and this can really help to move the play along.

I always think of those moments in a TV soap, when a character survives an explosion, or discovers that they're married to their long-lost twin:

MANDY: Long story. I'll tell you later.

And I always think 'what?!' If it was me, I'd be phoning up everyone I know to tell them. In story terms it's *interesting*, but it's no longer *dramatic*. It's stale.

The Passage of Time

The passage of time is another potentially awkward thing to convey on radio. In film and television the changing of the seasons or, indeed, the ageing of the central characters, is largely conveyed visually. Even in the theatre a change of costume can be used to suggest that time has moved on. But of course, on radio, we don't have that luxury.

Think carefully about the segue between scenes. In a radio play how do we tell the difference between spring and summer, for example? Or autumn and winter? How can we tell that two scenes don't run consecutively? Well, to be honest, it's difficult. We want to nudge the listener towards an understanding that time has indeed passed, without necessarily signposting the fact. We want to provide clues that lead to that conclusion.

We want to provide clues that lead to that conclusion. Often these will be non-verbal indicators. For example, music from an ice-cream van might usefully suggest summer, while the crack of exploding fireworks may help to conjure up an autumnal setting.

'Out' Lines

'Out lines' (the very last line at the end of each scene) must have punch. We need to continue to give the listener reasons to stick with the play. For example, imagine ending a scene like this:

F/X:	NESSA TAKES A SIP OF WINE.

| NESSA: | I probably shouldn't be drinking this.
(BEAT)
I might be pregnant. |

Music

Music is a useful way of indicating period and geographical location. It's also helpful in suggesting tone, and moving on the action of a play. And sometimes we might even be looking for a way to shake the listener out of a state of semi-stupor. Think of a short burst of music as a palate cleanser for the ears – if that isn't too jarring a mixed metaphor.

It can be difficult to get permission to play certain pieces of music on the radio. Using a track by ABBA or The Beatles, for example, can be decidedly tricky. To add further complication, due to recent copyright restrictions it's generally no longer possible to use more than three minutes of a track of music in the course of a play. This is frustrating if you want a specific passage of music to be used as a recurring motif throughout the play.

However, such restrictions can lead a writer and producer to make more creative musical choices, so always be open to suggestion.

Commissioned Music

Due to budget constraints, it's unlikely that a specially commissioned score will be produced for the production – it does still happen, but rarely. When it does, it can add a unique depth and texture to a play.

A Word about Exposition

Exposition is, as the word suggests, the way in which information is exposed in the course of a play. In theatre, film or television there are always visual indicators that can help the audience work out what is going on. In a radio play, time, place and character can only be created with the use of dialogue and sound effects. Sometimes, in order to orientate the listener, the signposting can be a little on the clumsy side to compensate for the fact that radio is a blind medium. The actor Timothy West beautifully pastiches the pitfalls of expositional writing in his spoof radio play *This Gun That I Have In My Right Hand Is Loaded*. Returning home from work Clive settles down for a drink with his wife, Laura:

CLIVE: Whisky, eh? That's a strange drink for an attractive, auburn-haired girl of twenty-nine.

The information imparted helps the listener to build up a mental image of Laura – but the joke (and I'm probably killing it dead by explaining it) is this: Clive knows what his wife looks like, and Laura knows what she looks like, so this information is being provided entirely for the benefit of the listener.

It's hard to maintain the balance between revealing too much information and too little; say too much and the listener no longer believes in the authenticity of the scene, say too little and you run the risk of baffling the listener.

On occasion I've been so anxious to avoid exposition that producers have asked me to put a few more clues back into the script to avoid bewildering the listener. There are often ways of slipping exposition under the radar. For example, an 'outsider' character who is unfamiliar with his or her surroundings is a positive boon. For example:

KEITH: Well, Alex, this is where you'll be
                          working. There's a pretty decent view of
                          the Shard…if you squint. Photocopier
                          over there…tea and coffee facilities
                          through that door on the left. Leo,
                          you haven't met Alex. Alex, Leo Harris.
                          One of our rising stars at Wilson-Stuart
                          Investments…

Don't Spoon-Feed Your Listener

In radio, the word 'exposition' is rarely used in a positive context. But actually, there are moments when a piece of information needs to be made explicit in order for the listener to keep up with the unfolding drama. I'll be honest, it's difficult to get through an entire radio play without falling back on some expositional device or other. But the truth is, the more information you provide, the more disengaged your listener will become.

'Bad' Language

If I'm reading a script destined for BBC Radio 4, and I see a 'shit' or 'fuck' on the first page I know there's trouble in store. I feel like a narrow-minded prude, suggesting that writers should lift 'shit' or 'fuck' out of their scripts. But I'll be honest, in most situations there's precious little chance of either of these words actually making it to air.

When I was a child, growing up in Cornwall, I often heard the word 'bugger' used, not in the pejorative sense, but to add colour to a conversation: 'I saw that old bugger come down the village', or 'funny bugger 'e was'. But use 'bugger' in a radio play, and incensed listeners will be dashing off letters of complaint before the credits roll. Many writers (and I daresay listeners) find this frustrating; feeling with some justification that it undermines the credibility of certain plays. Personally I'm inclined to think that swearing is part of the rhythm of life – it can add to the texture of good dialogue. In drama, as in life, there are certainly moments where only a 'fuck' will do, if you see what I mean? The trouble is there is no watershed in BBC radio.

But look at it this way. Imagine you've decided to use a flurry of swear words at the beginning of your script. Would you be entirely surprised if certain listeners decided that the play was not for them and chose to switch off the radio? I'm sure you wouldn't.

Imagine you decide to hold back – to wait a few minutes before you use a single expletive. This can change matters enormously. The listener is given the opportunity to connect with the characters – and suddenly it's that little bit harder to switch off the radio. If you can explain the reasoning behind your inclusion of an expletive it might well be enough to convince a producer that it's worth taking the risk to include it in the play. Your producer will then have to fill in a compliance form, which will explain the reasoning behind the inclusion of the expletive. These 'referable words' may be passed all the way up to the controller of the station who will make the final decision about whether or not the word can be used. This may all sound a little draconian to you. But unfortunately it's a fact of life in the world of radio drama.

There will be occasions when swearing might well be permitted. For example, moments of dramatic climax when it would seem puzzling if a character didn't respond with a well-chosen expletive. There are certainly times when it feels as though radio is out of step with the real world. I once had a long debate about whether or not we could insert 'penis' in the Woman's Hour slot. One of the problems is inconsistency. In the past I've been asked to cut the word 'bloody' from a nine p.m. Friday Drama, but I've heard the word 'fuck' used repeatedly in a radio documentary that was aired at 11 in the morning. To make things even more baffling, a risk that one producer might be prepared to take might never be contemplated by another producer.

I wish there was some way of being more definitive on this subject – but unfortunately, there isn't. It's frustrating because there's rarely any clear logic to it. I sometimes think (perhaps a little cynically) that the decision to allow this swear word or that swear word is often based on the relative rank of the playwright. A 'national treasure' might be able to get away with a fuck, whilst a less established dramatist might struggle with a wank, as it were. Be assured of one thing – it's unlikely that you'll be able to slip any bad language under the radar.

Swearing is allowing your character to lift the weight from the pressure cooker – it allows their true emotions to spill over. But there's also a downside to this. Releasing the imaginary weight can result in a dissipation of dramatic tension. Actually, if you deprive your characters of this outlet, you can sometimes crank up the tension of a scene.

The Evils of Product Placement

As a public service broadcaster the BBC is at pains not to provide product placement. However, I would argue that now more than ever we are defined by the consumer choices we make, and if we fail to take this into account in radio drama we risk writing quaint 'period pieces' which seem completely divorced from the real world. If a character says:

DAN: Yeah, I've just bought a new BMW.

It carries a different weight to the possible alternative:

DAN: Yeah, I've just bought a new sports car.

It communicates something else entirely, doesn't it? Of course, there are ways of making that second line less leaden – but I still think we'd feel the want of the BMW brand name. In the same way, which of the two following suggestions sounds more convincing?

GIRL: I'm goin down Burger King, you comin?

Or:

GIRL: I'm gettin a burger in town, you comin?

It's almost as bad as a character arriving in a bar and ordering a pint of 'non-specific'.

But listeners do get irritated if an innocuous piece of product placement slips through the net. I once had not one but two letters of complaint (from the same listener) for twice mentioning a UK department store in an Afternoon Drama.

Life After Death – Writing About Real People

From a strictly legal point of view, you can't libel the dead. What you can do is offend the living, especially if the representation of their nearest-and-dearest is controversial or unflattering. You may have slaved away for months, researching thoroughly to make sure your portrayal of the character is accurate – but if it's likely to upset living family members it can still cause trouble. Again, as a public service broadcaster, the BBC is particularly sensitive to criticism, and this has perhaps become more acute over the past few years.

Never Work with Children or Animals

Any animal can be added to the production with a simple flick of a switch. Not so with children.

Time is a precious commodity in studio and a chaperone will insist (and rightly so) that a child actor must be given frequent breaks, and this can severely hamper the schedule.

Of course, I'm not saying that you should exclude child characters from your play, but make certain that their presence is necessary.

Submitting a Script

It's often tempting to send out a script the moment it's completed. If humanly possible, hold back. Although we can never view our work with a truly objective eye, it can help to put the script to one side for a couple of weeks and forget all about it.

It's never a bad idea to print out your script so you have a hard copy to work from. Somehow, even in this technological age, I think a printed version of a draft gives you a better sense of the shape of your play than staring at a computer screen.

You have to prod and poke your script, analyse and interrogate, re-write and hone and when you think the play is as tight as it can possibly be then, and only then, will you have reached the end of the first draft.

Don't Discard Anything!

I'm a firm believer in never throwing anything away until your radio play has been recorded. Squirrel away each and every draft of your script – you never know when you might need to dust off and reinsert a previously discarded line of dialogue or even an entire scene.

Cut the First Five Pages …

It's often the case that the first few pages of a script offer little more than unnecessary set-up to character and situation. With an Afternoon Drama you've got 45 minutes at your disposal, so you need to make sure that you don't waste a single second. It's also worth considering cuts at the beginnings and ends of scenes – as any good party goer knows, it's always better to arrive late and leave early.

Editing a script can often free up the drama. Sometimes dialogue can seem too obviously 'complete' – or as a producer friend of mine bluntly (but accurately) puts it, 'it sounds like a line from a radio play'.

Less is More!

It's a sad fact that the sections of script to which a writer becomes most attached are often the first casualties of cutting. We often hang on to dialogue that could and should have been cut. Too often a capable writer undermines a script by trying too hard to impress. Never feel that your characters have to articulate every thought in their heads.

So begins the process of trimming back extraneous material. This is a stage that all writers go through and you're certainly not on your own here.

Delivering Your Script to the BBC

When you stop to consider that the BBC is the largest commissioner of radio plays in the world, you can perhaps appreciate the sheer volume of unsolicited scripts that are submitted every year. In BBC radio there is no literary department as such and most scripts are read by the producers themselves. Putting it in simple layman's terms, producers are overworked.

If you have already established yourself as a writer in another medium, make this clear – it can improve the chances of your work being read more quickly. But even if you're a less experienced writer, you don't want to give the producer reading your script the *impression* that you're an uninitiated novice. Keep your cover letter brief and to the point. Be clear about the intended broadcast slot for your play and avoid the following approach:

Dear Sir or Madam,

I feel confident that the attached script would be suitable for the Afternoon Drama slot. However, that said, I do think the script is quite funny, so I could easily edit it down by 15 minutes to make it fit a 30-minute comedy slot. Equally, if the premise of my play is considered dramatic enough to run to an hour I will happily go away and add another 15 minutes of dialogue/drama.

Yours faithfully,

Mr A. Writer

Similarly, you don't need to give the BBC advance warning that your script is on the way:

Dear Ms Producer,

I am currently working on a new radio drama, which I hope to send you in the next two or three weeks.

Miss A. Writer

Trust me, they can wait!

Allow the Script to Speak for Itself

There is no need to provide detailed character information when you submit your script. Anything that's vital for a thorough understanding of the drama should become obvious from the dialogue alone. A good, well-written play will distinguish you as a writer of promise.

How Long Will I Have to Wait before I Hear Back?

This is the difficult part, so steel yourself. It can often take anywhere from 18 months to two years for a producer to respond to an unsolicited script, and even then there's no guarantee that they'll be getting back in touch with good news. But what happens if a producer *is* interested in your script? Read on…

When is My Script Ready for Production?

Essentially, a script is not ready until your producer says it is. It can seem a depressingly long time between the first draft of your script and the polished, studio-ready version of the play. It's impossible to say how many drafts of the script you will produce before reaching the final, production-ready draft. It is, unfortunately, one of those 'how long is a piece of string?' questions. Often my scripts have run to four drafts after submission before being ready to be taken into studio – it could be more, it could be less. But I think four drafts is a good general rule of thumb.

When giving feedback, a sensitive producer will sugar the pill by talking-up what's good in the script before dealing with any structural issues which might be holding the play back. One thing a producer should never do is re-write your script. This happened to me on one occasion, and I was too green to know any better. I vowed never to let it happen again.

Finishing the Script

Sometimes a play seems to fall into place as if by magic, but I can't stress how rarely this is the case. All writers need to have some input from their producers – and some writers will need more editorial input than others. It's a lonely old process, sitting at a desk all day slaving over a hot computer, and every writer needs a measure of encouragement. But I'll be honest, there just isn't time for a writer to have their hand held every step of the way.

Don't let anybody try to convince you that your way of working is the wrong way. After all, it's the destination (i.e. the final production draft of the play) that's the important thing here – the route you choose to reach that destination is entirely up to you.

Once the script nears completion a producer might even ask you to come in for a meeting to read the play aloud. Don't worry; nobody's expecting you to be the next Sir Ian McKellen or Dame Judi Dench – it's simply about getting a sense of what the play might sound like when it's 'up on its feet.' I can quite understand that some writers may see this as a form of purgatory, but it can be incredibly useful – and also a lot of fun. Sitting down to tea and cake with my producer, we divvy up the parts and read through the script. It's an agreeably civilised way of working on a script. Not only do you get a more accurate sense of the length of the play (the producer may well time each scene on a stop watch), it's also easier to weed out 'problem lines'.

Try to be as objective as possible. Don't just make amendments because of your performance. You're a writer, not an actor. If sections of dialogue seem virtually unreadable, it's often because the speech is too formal.

Casting

> Actors don't have to learn lines and it doesn't matter what they look like.
>
> Simon Brett

It's often said that radio drama is a writer's medium – a sentiment that I wholeheartedly endorse. But it's equally true that it's an actor's medium. It's not a bad idea to write your play with specific actors in mind. I often do this, and even if my producer is not ultimately able to cast the actor I was writing for, it will almost certainly have helped in the creation of a rounded, three-dimensional character. So I try to build up a 'wish list' of suitable actors. If I go to the theatre, or watch a programme on television and I see an actor I like, I always try to scribble the name down, just in case.

Just flick through a copy of the *Radio Times* and look at the cast lists for the Afternoon Drama. The wealth of talent on show is often staggering. Even Hollywood stars have been known to take roles in radio plays every now and then.

As you may well have guessed, actors never take roles in radio plays because of the money. They do it for the love of radio. Compared to film or TV work, the daily rate of pay for even the most established performers is microscopically small.

It may seem that certain actors are employed on the radio with increasing regularity. Wisely, many producers will want to cast actors they have worked with before. Acting for radio requires a very specific technique, and it can take time to master the art. I have worked with actors who are completely new to radio, and valuable time can be wasted explaining technique to the uninitiated. This is something your producer could well do without.

There are certain actors who enjoy a reputation for being reliable and good to work with. Is it any wonder if producers want to work with them time and again?

Making the Offer

The producer or production coordinator will put in an offer to the actor's agent, which the agent will then accept or decline. Sometimes an agent will turn down a script without even passing it on to their client, so try not to take it personally if the role is rejected.

Even if an actor is technically available they may have decided to take advantage of down time between jobs by booking a holiday. This has happened to me on more than one occasion and it's frankly a bit depressing when it happens. Sometimes agents seem to have absolutely no idea what their clients are up to. An agent once claimed that an actress was available, only to discover a couple of days later that the client was actually in rehearsal for a stage play and therefore, obviously, *unavailable*.

It's sometimes helpful to do a little bit of research into who's doing what. Online, the Internet Movie Database (IMDB) gives a pretty exhaustive list of films and TV shows in production, and this can provide a hint about whether or not an actor might be free. I once discovered that an actor we were considering for a play was shooting four films simultaneously – needless to say, we didn't end up casting him.

Will There be a Reading before the Recording of My Play?

It's very rare to have a reading of a play before the first day of recording. It does still happen on occasion. But in 14 years of writing for the radio, I've only attended two such readings. Once for a technically complicated production involving a number of specially-commissioned songs, and once for a period drama in which it was essential that all of the cast spoke with the same distinct accent. It's a luxury – and one that can quickly eat into the production budget.

Before the Recording

You will almost always have an opportunity to tinker with your script before recording, even after the final version of the script, formatted by the production coordinator, has been sent out to the actors. As a wise producer friend of mine says, 'nothing is set in aspic'.

Of course, if you're making changes to every other line of your script it will inevitably cause delays in studio. And if your actors have been working on the script prior to recording (and we always hope they have been) they may be slightly frustrated to discover that everything's changed.

In the days leading up to the recording of your play, make sure you speak to your producer if you have any specific questions or concerns. Once you get into studio, there probably won't be time.

Though your script is complete, your work is far from over. Make sure you're as prepared as possible for the recording:

Checklist

1 Read back through your script before the first day of recording.

2 Highlight any sections of script that could be cut if the play overruns.

3 Check the pronunciation of any tricky words in the script.

4 Read back through your script one more time!

In Studio

| ACTOR: | We worked together a while ago. What were you playing? |
| ACTRESS: | I murdered your children. |

A 45-minute radio play will usually be recorded in two days (sometimes a day and a half). Now, two days may seem like an awfully long time, but let's break that down. You probably won't start recording until 11 o'clock on the first day of production (after a cast read-through of the script), you will stop for lunch at about 1 o'clock, picking up again at 2 and working through until around 6 o'clock in the evening. That's a grand total of six hours' recording time. There may be a brief coffee break in the afternoon to allow the actors time to breathe – which probably nibbles away another 15 minutes. Twenty minutes or more may be spent in the course of the day re-setting the studio between scenes. Ten minutes will be lost chasing actors into the studio from the green room. Another hour has flown by …

I'm not trying to make you anxious – but I want you to be clear before setting foot in the studio that time is not your friend. There, enough said!

Be Good to Yourself

When I had my first radio play produced, I booked myself into a very nice hotel a short stroll from the studio. I blew a large amount of my commission fee, but it was a pleasant introduction to a life in radio. I didn't have to negotiate buses or the Underground, and I arrived at the recording feeling well-fed and perfectly refreshed. Nowadays, living in London, I tend to treat myself to a decent breakfast on my way to the studio – it adds a sense of occasion to the recording!

Always Arrive Early

Unless you've arranged to meet your producer at a specific time, it's normally advisable to arrive at the studio half an hour before the start time that will be printed on the front page of your production-ready script, as sent out by the production coordinator. In the past I've often arrived too early, which has meant a long wait before the studio manager arrives to unlock.

Apart from getting yourself together before the recording and introducing yourself to your cast members as they arrive, there may be last-minute thoughts the producer wants to talk through – although usually this time will normally be spent making sure that the studio crew are up to speed.

The Read-Through

The first day of recording will generally begin with a cast read-through in the green room. It won't always be possible to gather the whole cast together for the read-through on the first day of a recording. For example, if an actor isn't needed until the second day, bringing them in for an hour on day one just uses up budget money that could be usefully employed elsewhere.

It's normally a pretty relaxed affair, with the actors sitting round with cups of tea and copies of the script. Each scene will be timed by the PC in order to give an approximate running time for the play. I will always sit with a pen or fluorescent marker and scribble over my copy of the script – highlighting lines that don't work and trying to identify any dead wood that can be stripped back if the play overruns.

A read-through isn't always a comfortable experience. Even after working on many different drafts of a script I never fail to be surprised (and by surprised, I mean shocked!). I have wandered dumbly from the green room, doubting every word on the page. But it's important not to panic if the read-through falls short of your expectations. In most cases the actors will be finding their way through the script – think of it as the warm-up before the performance.

Chances are you won't have time to discuss the play in much detail with your actors after the read-through – trust to the fact that most problems can be ironed out in the studio as you go, scene by scene.

There's precious little time to catch your breath before the actors move into the studio for their first scene and the production is up and running. As the actors head for the microphones, the writer and producer will make their way into the cubicle. More often than not, the writer sits at the producer's right hand, although this depends on studio layout. It has been noted that the writer is generally seated closest to the door (and read into that what you will!).

The desk is strewn with pages of script, fluorescent pens, biros, recording schedules (and revised schedules), coffee cups, packets of sugar, and an impressive assortment of biscuits (you will never eat more biscuits than during a radio recording).

You may have been given a recording schedule before you start recording, but it's much more likely that you'll be handed a copy on the morning of the first day in studio – this will help you keep track of the order in which scenes will be recorded. I always find it's useful to buy a loose-leaf clip file to hold my script in production – very handy for keeping documents like the printed schedule safely in one place.

My stomach gurgles continuously in studio – it's like listening to a malfunctioning coffee percolator. I sit at the desk in such a state of nervous tension that practically every internal organ goes into spasm. Imagine Rodin's *The Think*er but with furrowed brow and bottle of Rescue Remedy. That's me.

Incidentally, if you're awash with tea there will normally be time to nip out to the loo as the next scene is being set up. Choose your moment wisely!

Who is Responsible for Recording My Play?

In the past it was usual to have three studio managers (or SMs) working on a production. One SM would control the desk, speaking directly to the actors in studio. A second SM was responsible for any recorded sounds which were to be added during the recording (passing cars, birdsong, etc., etc.). A third SM was stationed in the studio producing spot effects (as discussed earlier). These days it's much more likely that you'll have two SMs working on the production – an SM on the desk, and an SM who operates both grams and spot effects.

Will the Scenes be Recorded in Order?

The speed of production can also be a satisfying aspect of the process. Come hell or high water, at the end of two days in the studio the play will have been recorded.

As is the case in film and TV, radio plays are rarely recorded in chronological scene-by-scene order – although, because of the rapid turnaround of radio, many producers will try to keep the recording as chronological as possible. This can certainly be useful for the actors as they deal with the emotional build of the drama.

If it's not practical to record chronologically, scenes will often be grouped together which take place in the same acoustic. For example, if the studio screens have been pushed together to stand in for the interior of a car.

Unless you have written long scenes, or scenes that are technically complicated (for example scenes requiring significant spot effects input – dinner parties, battle scenes, etc.) a producer will often try to record scenes in their entirety. This is generally the best use of studio time. However, if only a section of a page of script is to be recorded, the producer will normally give the actors a line number as a reference: 'We'll record from line 8 to 12 of page 52.'

Don't be upset if you discover an actor ripping apart your lovingly crafted script. Again, this is to prevent script rustle. It's not a value judgement on the quality of your play. The more papers an actor grips in his hand, the noisier it's likely to be and this will cause problems for the edit as the SM will have to spend time nicking out this infuriating rustling noise.

You may perhaps be familiar with film technique – the longueurs as scenes are set up, the endless retakes.

Not so in radio. Your producer and SM will be keen to get each scene recorded and completed as quickly as possible. The more time that's wasted on retakes the less time there will be to record later scenes in the play. In order to make full use of the time available, most SMs will record studio rehearsals as well as each take, just in case. Sometimes, but rarely, the actors will get it right first time.

Problem-Solving

At the risk of sounding like a scratched record, time (or lack of it) is perhaps the foremost consideration in the two days of recording.

It's important that the actors don't receive two sets of notes, as that can quickly cause confusion. Any notes on direction must come from the producer.

The producer will often want to talk to the studio to sort out quick-fix problems via the talkback (a microphone link between the cubicle and studio), before consulting with you. It's a good idea to wait until your producer's finger is off the button before you start giving feedback. With the advent of 'soft' buttons on the console desk it's often difficult to tell if the microphone is on – so if you can't think of anything nice to say, don't say it (or if you do have something negative to say, say it quietly!).

For longer notes or more complicated 'business' the producer will usually go through to the studio to talk to the actors in person. Most of the time the writer will remain in the cubicle during the recording – although for more fiddly bits of re-writing the producer will possibly ask you through to the studio. It's often simpler to talk through any re-writes or edits face-to-face with the cast, rather than dictating notes over the talkback.

A New Perspective

Often you will find that you have another slant on the play you've written. Actors and studio managers will frequently notice something that's slipped through the net – an inconsistency in the script, a factual inaccuracy, a section of dialogue that simply doesn't read as it should. Whilst this input can be incredibly useful, enabling you to view your script in a new and illuminating way, it can also be slightly bewildering at times. It's your script, and you should never feel browbeaten into making changes that you don't agree with. Actually, if you go along with too many suggested alterations it can have disastrous effects on the recording schedule. Remember, you and your producer are watching the clock, the actors are not.

Spreading

As previously discussed, the PC will have timed each individual scene in the read-through on the first day in studio. As the scenes are recorded, the PC will start to make another set of timings – a rough reckoning of the actual length of each scene. In almost all cases the recorded scene will be longer (sometimes significantly so) than when read in the greenroom – and this is known as 'spreading'.

I always think it's a good idea to check with the PC every so often to find out how each scene is spreading and the impact this is likely to have on the overall running time of the production. This will give you an indication of cuts you may need to make before the following day's recording, or during the edit.

If you are over-running and can see sections of text that might be usefully trimmed away, it's never a bad idea to make these cuts on the hoof. Actors will understand that time is a major consideration, and appreciate the need to make cuts here and there as they go along.

Check the order in which scenes will be recorded. Wherever possible, try to remain a scene or two ahead and make any necessary alterations in advance. It's never desirable to end up re-writing a scene as it's being recorded – this results in a lot of standing around as the writer makes tweaks and adjustments and adds considerably to the stress levels of everybody involved. Speed, as they say, is of the essence.

Do Take a Break …

By the time studio breaks for lunch you're likely to feel ten years older, and hungrier than you ever thought possible. It's usual to keep a civilised hour for lunch – although if recording is running considerably behind (it often is) then there might be a staggered lunch break for the actors. Even so, it's unlikely that the writer, producer, PC and SMs will have less than half an hour to eat and recover from the morning's session.

It's always sensible to get a bit of fresh air before succumbing to cabin fever. And who knows what opportunities your trip out of the studio might afford? I once nipped out for a sandwich and was served by a young man whose name badge said 'Skander'. As he typed in his ID code the name that flashed up on the till was 'Sandra'. Now, there's a little potted play in the making.

But it's advisable to return to your script as quickly as possible. I always think it's helpful to make the most of a lunch break to carry on working through the script to find possible tweaks. I like to take a few minutes when the actors have broken for lunch to have a wander round and contemplate matters. It may well be that any alterations you've made during the morning's recording session will have implications later in the script and you should try to stay on top of this.

Homework

Of course, you do have a good opportunity to go home after the first day of recording and spend time trawling through the remaining scenes before day two. Though if you're anything like me, when you do finally arrive home you'll be so exhausted from your day in studio that the last thing you'll want to do is spend more time looking at your script.

What if My Play is Under-Running?

I can't think of a more terrifying prospect than having to generate extra scenes on the spot in order to fill out a script which simply isn't long enough for the slot. This has only happened to me on one occasion – and I'm determined not to let it happen ever again. I read through the script on two separate occasions with the producer. Both readings came in at slightly over the allotted time for the slot, which would have allowed room for trimming in the edit to tighten the play. Only in studio did it become clear that there was a problem – the play was at least ten minutes shorter than the necessary 45 minutes. If a play is running slightly under then it's not a difficult problem to solve – music can be added, pauses between scenes can be opened up. If a play is ten minutes under there's nothing to be done except to add extra dialogue, and this is an experience that can chill to the very marrow.

The End of the Recording

As the afternoon of the second day approaches, so does the end of the recording.

Sometimes opening and closing credits, listing the cast, writer and producer, will be recorded in studio by one of the actors (though occasionally an in-house continuity announcer will drop in during the edit to record these announcements).

As the production winds down, your producer may well be checking with the PC to make sure that each scene in the play has actually been recorded before actors are released. This is not as acute a problem these days as it was in the golden age of radio when plays would often be broadcast live. There's a wonderful story of an actor leaving the studio early and, tuning in his car radio to listen to the remaining portion of the drama on his way home, he was seized by a nameless dread when he realised that he still had another scene to go. Thankfully, radio drama rarely goes out live these days.

And That's a Wrap

When I started out in radio, as soon as the recording was over, the actors, writer, producer and studio managers would beat a hasty retreat to the nearest hostelry to celebrate. It seems to happen less and less frequently these days and I firmly believe it's a tradition that needs reviving.

I was once so drunk after a recording that the producer had to escort me back to Waterloo Station to make sure I got onto my train (and didn't stumble beneath it). Happy days.

Outside Broadcasts

Outside Broadcasts (or OBs) can bring a depth of sound to the recording which would be almost impossible to achieve in studio. Chiefly for financial reasons, it's often not practical to record an OB outside London as the cost of transporting actors to and from the metropolis and the possible cost of overnight accommodation would be prohibitive.

It often used to be the case that OBs were cheaper than studio recordings. Unfortunately this is no longer the case, and it tends to be independent production companies who favour recording outside the studio.

The trouble with an OB is the difficulty of controlling the environment. I was once recording a number of scenes for an Afternoon Drama in London's Holland Park, contending with a persistent drizzle and the fact that we were unfortunate enough to be standing immediately beneath the flight path to Heathrow. If there's one thing that can hold up a recording, a low-level 747 must certainly be that thing. One of our poor actors was wandering up and down, light-heartedly bemoaning his lot. 'No wardrobe mistress!' he cried. 'No change of clothes! No caravan!' Matters were not much improved when we moved inside to record an interior scene. It sounded as though the ceiling was about to cave in. It turned out that a tap dance class was taking place immediately above us.

I once heard of an unfortunate producer who was out on a boat in the middle of the Thames, recording a play about trawler fishermen, only to discover that the recording coincided with a ceremonial flypast. But then, worse things do happen at sea.

The Edit

The date of the edit will be written on the cover sheet of the script, along with the transmission (or TX) date. Make a note of this date in your diary as soon as you receive the script.

A radio play that has been recorded over two days will most likely be allocated a two-day edit which will generally take place a week or so after the recording. Although the edit will often run over two consecutive days, that isn't always the case.

In most cases you will be welcome to attend, but if your producer would rather not have you sit in, do respect his or her decision. Inviting a writer to an edit is a courtesy and not a right. If you are invited to the edit, it's extremely unlikely that you'll be needed for the full two days. It's much more likely that the SM will assemble a rough cut of the production, which may well take a day to complete, before it's useful for you to come in to the edit suite.

When Are 45 Minutes Not 45 Minutes?

Actually, a 45-minute slot is not actually 45 minutes long. Nothing is ever that simple! Confused? Well let me explain. Your producer and studio manager (responsible for recording and editing the play) will attempt to get the play in at under 44 minutes. Ideally they'll be aiming for around 43 minutes and 30 seconds. Now, if you're new to radio, this may seem like quibbling over niceties – but this saving of time allows for opening and closing credits, and quite possibly a trail for a programme that might be going to air later that day.

An apparently alchemic-like process often takes place in the edit, adding a pace and tidiness to the performances that simply wasn't there in the recording. The listener would never know – and what's more, neither would the actors.

Are There Ways of Speeding Up the Recording So I Can Cut Less?

Yes, but only as a last resort if you're still struggling to shave all-important seconds from the finished production. There is a technological process known as 'Crunching', where the computer automatically tightens up pauses in the recording. It's not something that a producer or studio manager is eager to fall back on unless strictly necessary. If overused, it can result in the play sounding sped up.

The First Cut is the Deepest

Even if you're not needed in the edit, it's still quite possible that your producer will ask you to work back through the script to identify further cuts. When it comes to finding sections of the script that can be excised, it's helpful to find chunks that can be lifted without derailing the dramatic thrust of the play.

Be clear about the cuts you're proposing. Either use the page number and line number, or even email back the broadcast copy of the script, highlighting the sections of the script you think should be cut.

Will I Hear the Recording Before Broadcast?

You will always be given an opportunity to listen to the final, broadcast-ready version of your play ahead of transmission. In the good old days the BBC would send out CDs following the edit, but it's now more likely that you'll be provided with a link to download the play. Even if you've attended the edit, you should always listen back to the broadcast-ready recording. Realistically, the time for making changes has passed – but if there is a glaring omission or continuity flaw that no one picked up, do mention this to your producer. It might (I hardly dare utter this), just *might*, be possible to fix it.

I know a producer who once sent a dramatist the final edited recording of a play, but encouraged her to let him know if there was anything she was unhappy with. The writer emailed back to say how much she'd enjoyed the finished production, attaching a list of 50 ways in which it could be improved. The kindly producer was, you might say, hoist by his own petard.

Attendance Fee

'What is that?' I hear you ask. 'An attendance fee? Could it be that I'm entitled to an extra pot of money?' Well, yes you are – I've been keeping it up my sleeve as a little post-production treat. It's a small pot I'm afraid – at the time of writing it's considerably less than £100 per day of recording and is unlikely to increase any time soon – but think of it as a sweetener, securing your presence in the studio during production.

In most cases (especially if you're working in-house at the BBC) your attendance fee should be sent through automatically. Generally speaking, this sum of money will be paid to you (either as a cheque or, more usually, automatically transferred into your account) within a couple of weeks of the recording. If no money is forthcoming it's worth chasing the PC or producer, in case it's been overlooked.

What Happens Once the Radio Play Goes to Air?

Alas, often very little. I won't deny that it can be frustrating to work intensively on a script, sometimes for many months, only to discover that the play has been broadcast and it's all over with a whimper, not the hoped-for bang.

Far fewer column inches are dedicated to radio previews and reviews than was formerly the case and this is a real shame. It's also a wasted opportunity. The calibre of talent attracted to radio can be truly overwhelming, from world-class dramatists to the most celebrated actors. It must be said – and at the risk of being branded a cynic – having a star name or two in your cast makes the prospect of a preview or review considerably more likely.

The proliferation of digital TV channels is probably partly to blame for nudging radio off the printed page.

Gone with a Whimper?

It's certainly depressing to slave over a radio script, only for the resulting play to disappear into the ether without anything more than a one-line listing in the weekend TV and Radio supplements. These are the moments when even the most dedicated radio dramatist might stop to consider 'Is it really worth it?' This is a moment to remind yourself that the work is its own reward. Even so, I always like to trawl through the papers on the off-chance that the play *has* been previewed or reviewed. There are a number of dedicated and tenacious reviewers who work valiantly to keep the flag flying.

Can I Make a Living as a Radio Dramatist?

Writers are rarely attracted to radio with the hope of making their fortune. If they were, they would almost certainly be disappointed. For a couple of years in a row I was fortunate enough to make a fairly decent wage from radio writing. By this I mean I was able to feed and clothe myself and keep a roof over my head.

Most people would argue that it's impossible to make a living solely from writing for the radio.

Repeat Fees

Don't expect to receive much in the way of a royalty if your play is repeated. However, if you've had a number of repeats in the same year it's surprising how the money can mount up. With the advent of digital radio, your play may also see a life beyond Radio 4. I once discovered that a play of mine had been broadcast on a British Airways flight. It was one of the most exciting moments of my life. My radio play – airborne!

Sometimes there may even be a surprise review if your radio play is repeated, so always be on the lookout. Search through newspapers (particularly weekend TV and Radio supplements) and listings magazines, hunt for reviews on line – you never know what you might discover.

The Author's Licensing and Collecting Society (ALCS) collect repeat payments, which are then paid out via a writer's agent (or directly to an unrepresented writer). I command you – blow any money owing to you on fripperies. Go out for a (cheap) meal, buy yourself a new hat, go wild on Amazon. On no account must you spend this money on bills or pay it into a pension fund – have some fun, you've earned it. There, point made.

Can My Radio Play be Adapted for Another Medium?

There was once a tantalising moment when it looked as though one of my radio plays was going to be optioned by a film company, but alas, it came to nought. And I'm resigned to the fact that it will always come to nought. But it does happen. Radio plays have been turned into stage plays, and have even been used as the basis for TV dramas and screenplays.

Back to the Beginning

Once your first radio play has been broadcast, subsequent plays will almost certainly be sold on the basis of a synopsis alone; you will not be expected to submit an on-spec script. So how does a radio dramatist go about selling an idea?

How to Write a Synopsis

A synopsis provides an opportunity to begin shaping an idea that until now has only existed in your head. Best to think of it as a slightly elongated version of the blurb on a book dust jacket.

Some writers are better than others at writing a synopsis. In fact, I would say that writing a synopsis is an art form in its own right – condensing and crystallising an idea and turning it into a 'must have' offer.

It's difficult to make sure that you've covered all bases – so don't expect to get it right first time. After all, you're unlikely to know everything that happens in your play until you've written your play. I always think a synopsis is a statement of intent rather than a hard-and-fast route map.

In case you're wondering if you'll be paid for this development work, I'm afraid I'm going to have to disappoint you.

Pity the Poor Commissioning Editor

Imagine how many documents a commissioning editor has to wade through in each offers round – it's mind-boggling. So keep your synopsis succinct and to the point. Writing a radio synopsis is not like writing a synopsis for a screenplay, which may run to many pages. Don't waffle on or pad your synopsis out.

It's your job to convince the commissioning editor that your play should be commissioned. I'll go further than that – you need to make it clear that your play *has* to be commissioned.

So ask yourself the following questions:

1 Why write the play?

2 Why write the play now?

3 Why should *I* write the play (rather than any other writer)?

It's good to keep these questions constantly in mind as you're writing your proposal. First and foremost, the synopsis is a selling document.

Read back through the synopsis. Be honest, is it an idea that *you* would want to commission?

Here is an example of a recent synopsis I submitted for the Afternoon Drama slot, and which was successfully sold:

Hush! Hush! Whisper Who Dares!

By Christopher William Hill

London, 1969. The final preparations are underway at the Victoria and Albert Museum to mark the 90th birthday of E. H. Shepard with an exhibition of the illustrator's preliminary sketches for A. A. Milne's *Winnie the Pooh* stories. But as Shepard produces new illustrations of Winnie the Pooh for a revised edition of Milne's work, to be published by Dutton in the United States – the last he will ever draw – it becomes clear that he is rapidly going blind.

The guest of honour at the V&A exhibition will be the original Pooh Bear, on loan from New York City Public Library. But Christopher Robin's Pooh Bear is an imposter. The illustrations in the books are based on Shepard's son's much-loved bear – Growler.

Graham Shepard, the illustrator's son, was killed in 1943, when the ship he was serving on was torpedoed in the Atlantic. It is a death from which Shepard has never fully recovered, and the V&A retrospective and the new Dutton's illustrations have opened old wounds. A renewed press interest in the illustrator has further compounded matters.

Milne is long dead, and Shepard has begun to resent his association with the writer, who initially viewed Shepard as a 'perfectly hopeless' illustrator. But like a moth to the flame, Shepard returns time and again to Milne's characters, a chance to keep the memory of his son alive, trapped in a golden and perpetual childhood.

In the weeks preceding the opening of the V&A exhibition Shepard is once again reunited with Christopher Milne (the model for the fictionalised Christopher Robin), now fast approaching 50. Unexpectedly meeting in London, Shepard invites Christopher to his home in Sussex, on the edge of the Ashdown Forest – inspiration for Pooh's Hundred Acre Wood.

Norah, Shepard's second wife, is hopeful that the meeting of the two men will finally help her husband to recover from the death of his son. But the visit is more difficult than she could have predicted. Shepard finds it hard to relate to the adult Christopher Milne. Underpinning their relationship is the knowledge that unlike Graham Shepard, Christopher survived the war. To make matters worse, memories of the young Christopher Robin have started to displace memories of his own son.

But Christopher's life has also been blighted by his association with the eponymous bear, effectively destroying his relationship with his parents. Bullied throughout his childhood (fellow boarders would delight in quoting 'Hush, hush, whisper who dares? Christopher Robin's saying his prayers …') and dogged by the shadow of his infant alter-ego well into middle age, he has retired to the relative obscurity of his Dartmouth bookshop. He has not returned to the Ashdown Forest in years, where coincidentally, his estranged mother still lives.

Christopher cannot help but blame Shepard for the whimsical (and not altogether accurate) interpretation of his childhood – perpetuated once more in Shepard's new illustrations. If anything, Shepard's illustrations have had a more profound effect on Christopher than A. A. Milne's words – creating an idealised character that Christopher could never live up to.

Shepard struggles to complete his illustrations before a total loss of sight overtakes him. But does blindness offer an opportunity to retire into an untarnished world of his imagination, where Graham has never died and the Hundred Acre Wood is entirely untouched by the passing years?

Christopher has lost a father and Shepard has lost a son, and a surrogate relationship quickly grows between the two men. As the opening of the V&A exhibition approaches, are they finally able to forgive A. A. Milne for the shadow he has cast over both their lives, or is it just easier to keep alive the myth of a halcyon childhood that never quite existed?

With the publication of a new *Winnie the Pooh* book, E. H. Shepard is firmly back in the public's consciousness. In a recent auction, a collection of Shepard's illustrations of the eponymous bear sold for a staggering £1.26 million. Although the life of A. A. Milne and his relationship with Christopher Robin is well documented, the story of Shepard's relationship with his son has been sadly neglected.

Coming Up With Titles

A few years ago, for a friend's birthday, we visited the Royal Academy's Summer Exhibition where we devised the Royal Academy Game. This involved noting the number of a particular artwork on the wall, but giving it the title of whichever work was ten places further on in the catalogue, so number 53 was given the title of number 63, and so on. One painting in particular stood out. Acrylic on wood panel, it was a painting of a lone and stationary bumblebee. The painting, entitled *bombus terrestris*, was number 494 in the exhibition catalogue. Playing the game and flicking forward to exhibit number 594, the painting took on a far more ominous significance. The title? *'I assume a passive attitude and I wait'.* I always think it's best to come up with a title when pitching a play, rather than falling back on 'Untitled'. A title helps to give shape to the idea and can convey much about the tone and genre of your play. Ultimately, a title can be the deciding factor in a listener's decision to tune in or turn off.

Why are Plays Turned Down?

It can sometimes feel as though offers are being turned down for entirely arbitrary reasons. And in a sense, this is true. It could be argued that a commissioning editor's job is a necessarily negative one, finding cause to reject an idea rather than accept it. For example, 'There've been too many plays about the war recently,' or 'we've just bought an Afternoon Drama about opera.'

Sometimes you win and sometimes you lose.

It's important to be philosophical about this. If you can adopt a positive, 'laissez-faire' attitude, after a while rejection becomes like water off a duck's back. But nothing is ever wasted. Even if an idea is rejected, there's no saying that you can't re-pitch it at some point in the future.

Anniversary Plays

Remember that a play marking a specific anniversary (for example the birth or death of a significant historical figure) will almost certainly have been commissioned many months in advance of its transmission date. If you've realised it's the anniversary of Elvis's birth, imagine how many other writers have had exactly the same thought.

So think outside the box. Find obscure anniversaries that may slip through unnoticed.

Do I Need an Agent to Write for the Radio?

Don't worry if you haven't yet got an agent. The BBC issues a standard contract, negotiated with the Society of Authors and the Writers' Guild which offers protection to an unrepresented writer.

If you don't have an agent it's certainly worth becoming a member of the Writer's Guild or the Society of Authors – and even if you do have an agent it's still well worth joining.

How Will I Get Paid For a Commissioned Play?

Radio writers are paid by the minute. But don't get too excited – I should point out here that this fee is per minute of broadcast drama (45 minutes, 60 minutes, 90 minutes, etc.) and not the fee you're paid for every minute you spend *writing* the play.

If you are working in-house at the BBC, it is likely that you will be paid 50 per cent of the total fee on

payable on acceptance of the script for production (i.e.
when the script is ready to take into the studio).

The payment schedule may well be different if you
are writing for an independent production company
(or indie). It would not be unusual to receive half of the
fee on signature of contract, with the remaining sum
broken down into a further two chunks – a quarter of
the total fee to be paid on the first day of recording
and the final quarter to be paid on broadcast of the
play.

There is also a public service fee, which will again be
released on acceptance of the script. This is likely to be
no more than a couple of hundred pounds, but as my
father would say 'little fishes are sweet.'

Something to Focus the Mind

Almost as soon as a play is commissioned the writer
is given a transmission date, or 'TX DATE'. There are
flaws to this approach. Sometimes a play will be taken
into studio that could really benefit from another draft
(or two).

Be careful not to make unrealistic claims about how
quickly you will be able to deliver the first draft of your
script. If you need more time, talk to your producer.

The First Draft

I'm firmly of the belief that the initial draft of a script
is solely for the benefit of the writer. This is the first
time the story has been told, so who could realistically
expect you to get it right first time? Of course, you'll
want to make the script complete enough to convince

Writing for Radio

your producer that you haven't lost the plot (literally or figuratively), but you're still finding your way so don't expect to dot every i and cross every t.

But what if you're really not happy with the draft you've produced? It really is a waste of everybody's time if you send out your script before it's ready. A producer will often spend a considerable amount of time working through your script to offer detailed feedback. If the draft isn't working as it should, your producer will almost certainly be figuring out solutions to help you correct this. And if the script simply isn't fit to be read, your producer may well have been better employed working on another writer's script instead of yours.

What if My Idea Changes?

Naturally, the aim must be to honour the synopsis you originally submitted in the offers round – although obviously, if the script takes a different, but altogether more interesting path, nobody's going to hold that against you. It's always a sensible idea to keep your producer up to speed with any significant shifts from the synopsis as originally discussed.

The Writer–Producer Relationship

There now follows a correspondence which I include with the permission of Gordon House, an inspiring former Head of Radio Drama, and now a kind and forbearing freelance radio producer. He is a man to whose better judgement I almost always defer, and the only person, incidentally, I have ever witnessed slipping over on a banana skin.

Gordon will never pick up the telephone and shout and scream. Very gently, he attempts to coax out each successive draft of a play, using a finely balanced combination of flattery and coercion.

Hi G

You asked a while ago if I had any ideas that might be suitable for a series – I think you mentioned the Woman's Hour slot. There is something I've been mulling over for a while – 'Angarrack', about a Cornish stately home and gardens (late 1940s, early 1950s) that's being wound up (contents auctioned off) to be passed over to the National Trust (no son and heir, or there was one, but killed during the war). I'm convinced there could be a lot of mileage here …

Would be lovely to meet up for a cake and a chat at some point. We've got a new tea set – see, how can you resist?

All the best,

C

****

Tea would be irresistible. How are you fixed in the next two weeks?

G

Many a working relationship is secured over tea and cake. Here is the resulting pre-offer synopsis:

Angarrack

by Christopher William Hill

Cornwall, 1951. The Angarrack Estate, hereditary seat of the Penwerris family, is struggling in the age of post-war austerity. Sir Richard Penwerris has grown heartily sick of the Palladian wreck of a house, and dreams of retiring to a lodge house in the estate gardens. His younger wife, Helen, has no desire to let the house out of her grasp, and will do everything in her power to prevent its loss. But unbeknownst to Helen, Richard has already approached the National Trust and offered to bequeath the house to the nation. A clash of Titans ensues – with only one winner.

****

This will be both a cracking yarn (at one point Helen sets fire to the east wing of the house, with Richard risking life and limb to save his son) and a delightful black comedy. Christopher William Hill grew up in Cornwall, and has spent time on many large Cornish estates, so he is well qualified to write about them. The series will be fully dramatised, but with a smallish cast – there are three central characters: Sir Richard, his much younger wife Helen, and Richard's son, Rafe, whom Helen, suspicious of his intentions, sets out purposefully to seduce. The R4 audience will enjoy the classic dramatic dilemma of irresistible force meeting immovable object, embodied in the two large egos of Sir Richard and his wife.

This pre-offer gives a flavour of the drama. And if the commissioning editor's interest has been piqued, the writer and producer will sit down to concoct the full offer, which is a more detailed version of the original synopsis. This may well take into account issues of concern that have been flagged up by the commissioning editor. With cake and tea to fuel the discussion, I sat down with Gordon to work through problems in the synopsis and tease out the intended dramatic thrust of the series. So here is the full offer:

Angarrack

By Christopher William Hill

Cornwall, 1951. The Angarrack Estate, hereditary seat of the Penwerris family, is struggling in the age of post-war austerity. Sir Richard Penwerris, Bart., has grown heartily sick of the Palladian wreck of a house, which has hung as a millstone round the neck of his family for generations, and dreams of retiring to a lodge house on the edge of the estate. His younger wife, Helen, has no desire to let the house out of her grasp, and will do everything in her power to prevent its loss. Exhilarated by the heroic past of the Penwerris family, Helen has begun to pen a history of the baronetcy, deliberately turning a blind eye to the family's abundant foibles and peccadillos. But unbeknownst to Helen, Richard has already approached the National Trust and offered to bequeath the house to the nation. A black comedy.

Episode One

Spring, 1951. Helen has a grand scheme for Angarrack, planning to install electricity in the East Wing, which houses a priceless Rococo galleried library. But Richard, mired in debt, is struggling to keep up with his wife's costly restoration project. Behind Helen's back, he has already turned to the National Trust for help. Having failed to sire progeny, the family tree is withering on the vine, until Rafe, a charismatic artist, arrives at Angarrack, claiming to be Richard's son and heir.

Episode Two

Summer, 1951. Although illegitimate, Rafe is welcomed with open arms by his contrite father. Suspicious of Rafe's intentions, Helen sets out to seduce him. It soon becomes clear that Rafe is emotionally unstable, prone to depression and delusion. As a relationship blossoms between Rafe and Helen, she believes she can convince her malleable stepson to side with her and prevent Angarrack's acquisition by the National Trust. But Rafe's motives are entirely innocent. He has no intention of inheriting, and can see the sense in his wayward father bequeathing the house. As the National Trust descends on the estate, Helen views her husband's actions as the betrayal of a once-proud Cornish baronetcy.

Episode Three

Autumn, 1951. As Helen reluctantly plans for the move to the Lodge House, Richard begins to auction off personal family items to raise funds. But as public interest is aroused in the more colourful aspects of Penwerris family history, Helen is furious that Richard's actions have led to the airing of dirty linen, especially as it conflicts with her own 'authorised' version of the family's apparently glorious past. As Helen's world seems to collapse around her, and her social stock slips, a chink of light appears. It becomes clear that the National Trust would never have considered taking on Angarrack House but for the presence of its unique Rococo library.

Episode Four

Winter, 1951. Desperate to stave off the National Trust's acquisition of Angarrack, Helen resorts to drastic measures. Convinced that the loss of the library will be enough to stop the Trust in their tracks, she plans for the limited destruction of the East Wing. Turning to Daphne Du Maurier's *Rebecca* for inspiration, Helen is certain that a fire will be blamed on the new electrical re-wiring (a cause of devastation in more than one Cornish stately home). Wrongly believing that Rafe is trapped inside the burning house, Richard is killed attempting to rescue his son. With the fire doused by the inclement Cornish weather, arson is detected and the finger of suspicion points at Helen.

Episode Five

Spring, 1952. Rafe has inherited Angarrack, and plans are in motion for the official handover to the National Trust. With only circumstantial evidence to link Helen to the fire, no charges have been brought. Relations have cooled between Rafe and Helen, who is forced to retreat to the Lodge House. But rumours abound that the fire was not accidental, giving rise to Rafe's paranoid belief that he was responsible for his father's death. Helen senses her opportunity, and when Rafe turns to her for help she's only too happy to encourage her stepson's fantasies. With Rafe found guilty of manslaughter and no remaining family member in line to inherit Angarrack, the estate is Helen's to do with as she pleases. And it doesn't please her to give away the house to the National Trust. Alone at last inside the crumbling Palladian edifice, the history of the Penwerris family is hers to write entirely at her whim.

With *Angarrack* successfully sold, I went away to write the series, with Gordon providing helpful feedback as I completed each draft.

Dear Christopher

Great to see you yesterday and cake was just what I needed. And scones too!

We're going to have a very enjoyable Woman's Hour – and Ep 5 now very much in the right direction. I like the idea of Helen & Tregunna inextricably yoked together by their both having incriminating info on the other.

We've agreed:

– that Tregunna burns the library down by accident; you're going to 'seed' more examples of his clumsiness/ frailty in earlier episodes

– that Tregunna is happy for Rafe to take the rap as he deeply disapproves of the young heir sleeping with his stepmother (and it gets him off the hook!)

– You'll 'seed' more examples too of Rafe's nervous illness (bit of research here?)

– We also need to make clear that for all her immoral duplicity, Helen – like Tregunna – has a genuine love of Angarrack and what it stands for; her husband just wants a quiet life, the money, a bit of shooting and his train set.

– One could suggest a bit more too, perhaps, that one of the reasons Helen seduces her stepson (alongside her own boredom and sexual dissatisfaction) is to get one up on Ralston from the National Trust, who could perhaps have an attempted seduction scene of his own?

– You'll do a bit of modest pruning of Eps 1 and 2.

– And you'll have new drafts for me by Friday 9th September.

All very best – and thanks again

Gordon

With each of the five episodes completed it was time to trim and tighten the series to make quite certain that it would fit the allotted time slot. As previously discussed, when editing it's often useful to look for larger chunks or even whole scenes that can be lifted without resorting to the fiddly and time-consuming job of cutting lines here and there throughout the script. The following scene was cut entirely – can you tell why?

SCENE ONE: INT. HALLWAY. DAY.

HELEN: (ENTERING) It's a deluge out there.
F/X: HELEN'S VOICE ECHOES IN THE CAVERNOUS HALL. DOGS SHAKE OFF WATER.
Monty! Stop it!
TREGUNNA: The fire's lit in the morning room.

F/X: HALL CLOCK CHIMES.

HELEN: Marvellous. Can you rustle up sandwiches, Tregunna?

| TREGUNNA: | Luncheon meat? |

| F/X: | HELEN WALKS THROUGH TO MORNING ROOM. |

| HELEN: | Splendid. Absolutely ravenous. |

It's a brisk opening scene, but does it tell us much about the characters? Well, no, not really. It's unnecessary pre-amble and we can do without it.

Consider the following scene. Does it serve a more necessary dramatic function?

SCENE EIGHT: INT. GALLERY CORRIDOR. DAY.

| F/X: | HELEN, RICHARD AND RAFE WALK BRISKLY ALONG GALLERY CORRIDOR. |

| RAFE: | The paintings … they're all— |

| HELEN: | Family? Yes. |

| RICHARD: | The rogues' gallery. |

| RAFE: | Who's that? |

| HELEN: | Sir Pelham Penwerris. Even by seventeenth century standards the man was no oil painting … not even in his own oil painting. |

| RAFE: | Ironic. |

| HELEN: | Isn't it. And artists tended to compensate, didn't they? |

RAFE: Compensate?

RICHARD: For a face like a slapped arse.

RAFE: Yes. I suppose. (IMPRESSED) I like that.

HELEN: It's Gainsborough. School of Gainsborough. I'm not entirely—

RAFE: Who is it of?

HELEN: The second Viscount Penwerris.

RAFE: How did he end up? Happily, unhappily—?

HELEN: We all end up unhappily. It's a question of how long we can stave off the inevitable.

RICHARD: That's your grandfather … the fourth Viscount.

HELEN: Queen Victoria visited him once.

RICHARD: Tried to. There was no one here. She went away again.

HELEN: At least she *came*.

RICHARD: The plasterwork is allegorical, so they tell me. Eden … or Gethsemane … blazes only knows. I never read the Bible. Too much sex and violence.

HELEN: Sex?

RICHARD: Begetting. That's sex, isn't it?

HELEN: Dinner, says she with a heavy heart.

RAFE: Oh …

HELEN: We don't dress for dinner
                    anymore. Only at Christmas and State
                    funerals.

RICHARD: Three pointer.

RAFE: What?

HELEN: The decapitated stag …

RAFE: Where?

HELEN: Over yonder … leering down from on
                    high …

RAFE: (LOW) Good God …

RICHARD: Shot that one myself.

HELEN: Travelled all the way up to Scotland to
                    slay it, didn't you, darling?

RICHARD: Gave it a sporting chance.

HELEN: It could hardly shoot back.

RICHARD: You're too sentimental.

HELEN:	Mustn't complain, I suppose. If Richard didn't go out shooting, it'd be Spam three times a week.
F/X:	<u>CREAK FROM ABOVE.</u>
	Watch out!
RICHARD:	Incoming!
F/X:	<u>PIECE OF MASONRY CRASHES TO EARTH.</u>
RAFE:	(SHAKEN) Bloody hell …
HELEN:	Yes. You'll get used to that.
RAFE:	I could've been—
HELEN:	Killed. Yes.
RICHARD:	(BARKS A LAUGH)
HELEN:	Pays to keep your wits about you.

So what was the function here? The scene established the fact that Richard was the hunting, shooting and fishing type, which helped to clarify one specific aspect of his character and explained the profusion of taxidermy later referred to in the script – but it did little more than that. In simple plot terms, it didn't actually help to advance the story. And if detail adds colour but fails to contribute to the plot, then it really can be underlined as a possible cut. So consider the following scene.

SCENE TWO: INT. BILLIARD ROOM. NIGHT.

HELEN: Tregunna … is that clock right?

TREGUNNA: It's losin'.

HELEN: Well wind it, can't you?

TREGUNNA: 'is lordship used to wind it.

HELEN: Unless it's escaped your notice—

TREGUNNA: 'is lordship 'ad the knack.

HELEN: You can pack away the railway set.

TREGUNNA: But … Sir Richard's railway …

HELEN: Does *everything* have to be an
                argument?

F/X: <u>MONTY HOWLS MOURNFULLY.</u>

TREGUNNA: Dogs know.

HELEN: I daresay they do.
                (BEAT)
                Well?

TREGUNNA: You ab'm given instruction.

HELEN: About what?
                (BEAT)

TREGUNNA: Sir Richard's gonna be laid out in the
                breakfast room, is 'ee?

HELEN:	What?
TREGUNNA:	All the estate … they godda pay their respects.
HELEN:	Yes, but by all accounts Richard looks rather like some poor creature you've dragged out of the oven.
TREGUNNA:	It's tradition.
HELEN:	It's not my tradition. Good god … if there's one thing guaranteed to put us off our food it's a corpse lying in the middle of the breakfast room.
TREGUNNA:	Old ways.
HELEN:	Disgusting ways.
TREGUNNA:	Thass as maybe.
HELEN:	If you're that concerned, why don't you just sweep out the fireplace and empty the ash into a box? You can carry it round the estate … everyone can have a peek inside. No one'll be any the wiser.
TREGUNNA:	Iss about respect.
HELEN:	Good God. Spare me the sermons.

This was a much more painful cut to make. The scene helped to reveal the tension between Helen and Tregunna and therefore had a useful dramatic purpose.

However, as there were other scenes in the episode that also conveyed this tension, a sacrifice had to be made.

With the script tweaked and refined, it was ready to record. Time to consider the next project!

So, What Slots Are Available to Me?

In recent years the number of production slots available to writers has been cut back considerably. The Friday Drama for example (attracting an audience of around 300,000 listeners), afforded an opportunity to challenge the listener in ways that perhaps the Afternoon Drama cannot. *The Wire*, on BBC Radio 3, was another slot that set out to challenge the listener. Alas, this has also been cut from the schedule.

Afternoon Drama

Broadcast every weekday afternoon, the Afternoon Drama is the bedrock of BBC Radio 4's drama output. The plays occupy a slot of 45 minutes, which equates to around 7,500 words of script (including all dialogue and F/X notes). In terms of genre it caters to most tastes. It attracts first-time radio writers as well as the most established of dramatists.

Saturday Drama

The Saturday Drama, broadcast weekly on BBC Radio 4. It's similar in form to the Afternoon Drama, with a clear emphasis on plot, but it does give the writer 15 minutes of extra airtime in which to flex the creative muscle. At 60 minutes in length, this is approximately 10,000 words of script (including all dialogue and F/X notes). The slot is unlikely to be the first port of call for an inexperienced radio writer.

15 MINUTE DRAMA

The 15 Minute Drama is broadcast on weekdays on BBC Radio 4. In the morning it's embedded in the magazine programme *Woman's Hour* and is then repeated the same evening. Each episode will be approximately 2,500 words in length (including all dialogue and F/X notes). Although the focus is on original drama, the slot is often used for book adaptations. Again, it would be an unusual entry-level slot for the novice radio writer.

Other stations also commission new drama – BBC Radio 3 in particular having the flexibility to commission plays of up to 90 minutes in length (roughly equivalent to a full-length stage play or screenplay). This provides a wonderful opportunity for a writer to expand on an idea that might seem pinched as an Afternoon Drama or Saturday Play. This is by no means an exhaustive list of available radio slots – it's merely intended as an appetiser. Commissioning guidelines for drama on Radio 4 and Radio 3 are published online – so do explore the available possibilities.

CLASSIC SERIAL

The Classic Serial, devoted to serialised book adaptations, is a Sunday afternoon slot on BBC Radio 4. Each episode is an hour in duration – again, equating to approximately 10,000 words of script. Though this slot is perhaps geared towards a more established radio dramatist, once your first play has been broadcast it's certainly worth consideration.

Adaptations – Do Your Research

Search online to see if a book has already been adapted for the radio. If a book has recently been re-issued it's more than likely that another writer has also thought of adapting it for radio.

Even if a book has been adapted for radio in the past, there's no saying it can't be adapted again with a new spin and a fresh perspective. Talk to your producer as they may well know which books are being considered for adaptation, and will be able to find out which books have already been adapted.

Obviously, books which are no longer in copyright will be cheaper to adapt than last year's best-seller.

Making an Adaptation Relevant

Often there will be a fair amount of cleaning up to do, to make the dialogue relevant to a contemporary listener. Avoiding the temptation to turn the dramatisation into an out-and-out period piece is always tricky. Similarly, there can be dangers in making a dramatisation too edgy and contemporary.

I always feel a certain responsibility to listeners who may well be tuning in because they have a genuine affection for the original book. Wherever possible I want the listener to have a comparable experience to picking up the book and reading it. If you can cut back and dramatise the book without the listener feeling that anything has been excluded, then I think you can consider this a little victory.

When it comes to a very familiar novel you perhaps have license to be more creative in your adaptation. With a lesser-known work, I would always try to present the adaptation as faithfully as possible.

What Makes a Book Suitable for Adaptation?

I prefer to think that all books are suitable for adaptation – though perhaps some are more readily adaptable than others.

Henry James's *The Turn of the Screw* is an excellent case in point of an ideal story for radio.

The Turn of the Screw

A governess is sent to look after two infant charges. It seems to the governess that the children are haunted by two ghosts – but who has seen what?

On radio it's perfectly possible to be as enigmatic as the original story. You can leave the listener to determine the 'truth' of the tale. Are the ghosts real, or are they simply the product of a fevered imagination? In most cases, if the book was to be adapted for a visual medium, it would be necessary to make a distinct choice about this. But radio allows for a lot of trickery, misdirection and subversion. It's like Schrödinger's cat. On radio, the cat can be both dead and alive unless the listener decides to think otherwise. You can confound all the listener's assumptions.

With radio it is sometimes possible to have your cake and eat it.

Is it My Responsibility to Check if a Book is Available for Adaptation?

It's never the responsibility of the dramatist to chase rights availability; this will always be left to the BBC contracts department.

Adaptations are often pitched in an offers round without first checking whether the rights to the original work are available. This might seem a peculiar way of going about things, but imagine how irritated an agent would become if they were constantly approached for rights availability only to discover that the dramatisation was then turned down at the offers stage.

If you're successful in selling the adaptation in an offers round it's best to hang fire until you're certain the rights have been secured. Even if there's a verbal agreement to release rights, you're better off waiting until everything has been signed, sealed and delivered before beginning work. I once had a shaky few weeks when I'd been working intensively on a dramatisation that had to be been turned around fairly swiftly for an impending recording date, only to discover that there were still unresolved rights issues. The only thing to do was down tools and sit on my hands until we were eventually given the green light and I could carry on.

Matters become even more complicated when it comes to foreign rights. In effect, the BBC will be paying for two sets of rights: to the writer of the original book, and also to the translator. This can prove prohibitively expensive.

Continuity

If your adaptation is split over two or more episodes, you may well be asked to write a continuity announcement which will help to re-orientate the listener. For example, the following intro was used to bridge a two-episode adaptation of Stella Gibbons' *Nightingale Wood*:

> CONTINUITY: And now the conclusion of our Classic Serial, *Nightingale Wood,* Stella Gibbons' pre-war comedy of manners. The widowed Viola, ensconced in Essex with her stifling in-laws, finally has the chance to escape to Stanton-on-Sea on holiday as Mr and Mrs Wither travel to the Lake District to take the cure. Still pining for the dashing and debonair Victor Spring, Viola is desperate for something exciting to happen. But Viola's sister-in-law Tina seems to have more pressing matters on her mind – her steadily and conveniently ailing friend Adrian Lacey …

How Will I Be Paid for a Radio Adaptation?

The payment for radio adaptation is staggered, depending on how much work will be needed to dramatise the original book. Some novelists supply so much dialogue that the task of adapting the work is a relatively straightforward one. Sometimes you'll have a lot of cleaning up to do. There's often a marked difference between dramatic dialogue and prose dialogue.

A serialised dramatisation of a long Russian novel can keep a dramatist warm long enough to survive the harshest of Siberian winters.

Coming Up with an Idea

So how do we think up ideas for radio plays? Often a plot builds incrementally over weeks or months and can be informed by any number of sources; newspaper or magazine articles, snippets of overheard conversations, or even the tall tales of friends and family. An idea ferments and brews then slowly, over time, a plot is born.

I'd wanted to write a radio play about a conductor for some time, but was struggling to find a plot structure. One afternoon I was reading a newspaper article about conductors who had died conducting Wagner's *Tristan und Isolde*. As an incurable hypochondriac, I couldn't help thinking how difficult it might be for a conductor if similarly afflicted, with the weight of a 'cursed' opera pressing down on his shoulders … you see how quickly things begin to fall into place? When it came to casting the completed play things seemed to click in an equally efficient way. It was one of those very rare occasions where every actor we'd placed on our 'wish list' was miraculously available for the recording.

We were fortunate enough to have a very musical studio manager, who was able to stand in as the rehearsal pianist. We also needed a singer who felt confident enough to tackle a Wagnerian aria – no mean feat, but we did it. For a play about fate, it appeared that the gods were smiling on us.

Killing Maestros was recorded over two days. I have to confess at this point that the script you are about to read was not quite the script we recorded. Agonisingly, we discovered in the edit that the play was 15 minutes too long. It was a painful process to cut so much text – but needs must!

KILLING MAESTROS
A play for radio
By
Christopher William Hill

FIRST BROADCAST: 14th AUGUST 2003

CHARACTERS
KARL LIEBERMAN – New York, mid 40's.
RUTH LIEBERMAN – New York, early 40's.
SERGEI BODANOV – English, early 50's.
LAURA VAN HELDEN – English, mid 40's.
EMILE DAENEKER – English, mid 40's.

London, present day.

F/X:	PHONE RINGS. A CLICK AS THE ANSWERPHONE KICKS IN.
SERGEI:	You've reached Sergei Bodanov. Unfortunately, I'm not here to take your call, but if you leave your name and number after the tone, I'll endeavour to get back at you.
F/X:	A SHRILL ANSWERPHONE 'BLEEP'.
EMILE:	(D) Sergei, this is Emile. If you're there, pick up the phone. (PAUSE) Sergei? *Please* pick up the phone. Look, I don't know if you're in London or out of the country, but … Sergei, it's Max. He's dead.
GRAMS:	AN EXCERPT FROM THE OVERTURE TO WAGNER'S *TRISTAN UND ISOLDE*.

INT. LIEBERMAN'S OFFICE. DAY.

F/X: THE QUIET HUM OF TRAFFIC FROM OUTSIDE THE OFFICE.

SERGEI: Emile Daeneker phoned to tell me Max had died. I was out at dinner, ironically just around the corner from the Royal Opera House. They'd been in rehearsal.

LIEBERMAN: You were very close to Max?

SERGEI: We trained together. In Paris. The Conservatoire. He was a year older than me.

LIEBERMAN: And his lifestyle … ?

SERGEI: Unrelentingly masochistic. I would eat croissants, Max would only eat apples. He didn't like rich food. Salads. He lived on salads. I think he was the first vegetarian I ever met. It made him very unpopular with the French. I would eat croissants and read. Max would go jogging. When we were conducting, that was different. That was my exercise. But Max? Max would train for hours in front of the mirror. Holding his baton. It wasn't some narcissistic character flaw, although God knows he had that as well. It was the pursuit of perfection. When he died … the suddenness …

LIEBERMAN: Tell me what happened, Sergei.

SERGEI: They think Max was dead before he hit the floor. Heart attack. The BBC were filming rehearsals for *Tristan und Isolde* at the Royal Opera House. A retrospective of the life and work of Max Blom, although in retrospect their timing could have been more opportune. I keep watching the video … they allowed me to take a copy. I wanted to see it before I took over as conductor. Before I *replaced* him.

LIEBERMAN: But surely, Sergei. You had a choice. They could have found another conductor to replace Max Blom?

SERGEI: A moth to the flame.

LIEBERMAN: An obligation to your friend? An act of remembrance?

SERGEI: More than that, Doctor. It was divined by Providence.

LIEBERMAN: Providence?

SERGEI: My father was a Russain émigré, I have a deeply ingrained sense of fatalism. I *had* to conduct the opera.

LIEBERMAN: But Max … ?

SERGEI: I've watched him die a hundred times. Pu-pu-pum. He clutches at his chest, and bang. *Salute Maestro*. The second bassoonist marked a cross in his score at the eighty-ninth bar of Act Two, and notes, 'here dies Max Blom, Maestro'. Melodramatic of course, but I'm afraid that's symptomatic of bassoonists. (PAUSE) I have six weeks, Doctor Lieberman. Six weeks before the first preview performance. Six weeks to get to the root of this 'evil' ... I use the word advisedly –

LIEBERMAN: Psychotherapy is an inexact science, Sergei.

SERGEI: Six weeks for you to *cure* me.

GRAMS: A FURTHER EXTRACT FROM THE OVERTURE TO *TRISTAN UND ISOLDE*.

LIEBERMAN: Sergei, in our last session you spoke about superstition. The *superstitions* surrounding certain operas—

SERGEI: When it comes to doom-laden opera, *Tristan* is about as good as it gets. Or as bad as it gets, depending on your point of view—

LIEBERMAN: Go on.

SERGEI: … I hadn't stopped. Quite apart from the onstage deaths (there are four, including of course our eponymous hero and heroine), the incidental deaths are simply staggering. The *offstage* deaths. George Ander was due to play Tristan in the first production

of the opera, but went mad and was
replaced by Ludwig Carolsfeld who
died shortly after the premiere. The
conductors Felix Mottl and Joseph
Keilberth expired while conducting the
second act. And now, Max Blom. All
things considered, Doctor, *Tristan und
Isolde* is not the happiest of operas.

LIEBERMAN: But you say it was more than this. More
than just *coincidence*?

SERGEI: The subject matter, you see?
Doomed love. It's very hard not to be
superstitious where doomed love is
concerned. There are exceptions to the
rule. I conducted *Traviata* for the New
York Met in '93. Violetta at least has
the good grace to die of tuberculosis.
Something conventional. There's no
witchcraft in it.

LIEBERMAN: Witchcraft?

SERGEI: I'm talking in the most general sense.
The supernatural. Max was not killed by
witchcraft.

LIEBERMAN: No. Of course not.

SERGEI: Max was killed by Richard Wagner.

GRAMS: ANOTHER EXCERPT FROM THE
               OVERTURE TO TRISTAN UND ISOLDE.

               EXT. HAMPSTEAD HEATH. DAY.

F/X:	<u>LIEBERMAN AND LAURA TALK AS THEY WALK THROUGH THE PARK. TRAFFIC CLOSE BY. A BUSKER PLAYS AT A DISTANCE.</u>
LAURA:	Karl, you know what my advice would be—
LIEBERMAN:	Yes, I know.
LAURA:	My *professional* advice.
LIEBERMAN:	Laura—
LAURA:	If you don't want to listen there are lots of other therapists you could talk to.
LIEBERMAN:	I want to talk to *you*
LAURA:	I don't know whether to laugh or cry. It's like being back at university.
LIEBERMAN:	You always took time out then.
LAURA:	I'd never met an American before. You were exotic. Hampstead was such a haven of peace and tranquillity until you came back, Karl. So, your client. He's haunted by Wagner? The composer?
LIEBERMAN:	Of course the composer. You see, this is my luck. This is the way God taunts me.
LAURA:	God is dead, Karl. A symptom of collective hysteria. Have you eaten? I've only got a few minutes.

LIEBERMAN:	I take on a new client. Is it something straightforward? Agoraphobia? Low self-esteem? No. I take on a client and he's haunted by an anti-Semite. One day a patient will walk into my office and tell me he's haunted by … I don't know, someone kosher. George and Ira Gershwin, Gertrude Stein … Woody Allen—
LAURA:	A neurotic haunted by a neurotic? Anything else? Any other symptoms?
LIEBERMAN:	The Wagner thing isn't enough?
LAURA:	Well … ?
LIEBERMAN:	There's a tendency towards …
LAURA:	Yes?
LIEBERMAN:	… Hypochondriasis.
LAURA:	Obsessive-compulsive?
LIEBERMAN:	Yes, but—
LAURA:	A red letter day. Congratulations! God, is that the time?
LIEBERMAN:	You're laughing.
LAURA:	I'm not.
LIEBERMAN:	Your mouth is twitching.

LAURA: Facial tic. Karl, I've got to get back. I've got a client in ten minutes—

LIEBERMAN: We haven't even skimmed the surface—

LAURA: There's more? Don't tell me, he's afraid of heights … pigeons. Look, take my advice. As a friend, even if you don't listen to me as a consultant. Drop him. Life's too short.

LIEBERMAN: This is interesting.

LAURA: Interesting? Have you ever met an interesting hypochondriac, Karl? Honestly?

LIEBERMAN: … Different then. The case is *different*.

LAURA: Okay, okay.

LIEBERMAN: The hypochondria is just the tip of the iceberg. The Wagner fixation … that's something new.

LAURA: New? In what way?

LIEBERMAN: It's an *inherited fixation*.

LAURA: Right, an inherited fixation. Some kind of hereditary … Teutonic … *yearning*? Or am I missing something?

LIEBERMAN: Inherited was the wrong word. *Passed over*. Somebody else's neurosis … a *specific* neurosis … has somehow manifested itself in his mind. I think that's fascinating.

LAURA: Okay.

LIEBERMAN: Laura, he senses the *presence* of Wagner.

LAURA: So what is this? Some kind of auditory hallucination?

LIEBERMAN: I don't know what it is.

LAURA: Refreshingly candid for a psychotherapist.

LIEBERMAN: It's too early yet.

LAURA: So, if this is an inherited fixation …
if he's taken on somebody else's hallucination … you'll stop me if I'm getting this wrong … who's it inherited from?

INT. LIEBERMAN'S OFFICE. DAY.

SERGEI: I hadn't seen Max for four, five months maybe. We met on the South Bank … outside the Festival Hall.

LIEBERMAN: When was this?

SERGEI: I suppose a month … six weeks before he died. He was different.

LIEBERMAN: Different? How?

SERGEI: Distracted. Normally we'd meet for
               lunch, the Dorchester perhaps. Or
               White's.

LIEBERMAN: But you met outside the Festival
               Hall?

SERGEI: He didn't want to go inside. He kept
               pacing … he wanted to walk. He must
               have lost a stone in weight, and for a
               man as sinewy as Max, it gave him a …
               sunken look. Haunted.

LIEBERMAN: Haunted?

SERGEI: He was constantly looking around
               him, as if he was *expecting* someone.
               And then a most peculiar thing
               happened …

LIEBERMAN: Yes?

SERGEI: My mobile began to ring.

LIEBERMAN: And?

SERGEI: I reached into my pocket to get the
               phone and … and Max wrenched it
               from my hand and hurled it into the
               river.

LIEBERMAN: Did he offer an explanation?

SERGEI: I *demanded* an explanation.

LIEBERMAN: And?

SERGEI:	He said he was sure … *convinced* it was Richard Wagner.
LIEBERMAN:	On the mobile phone?
SERGEI:	On the mobile phone. On *my* mobile phone.
LIEBERMAN:	What did you do?
SERGEI:	What could I do? I laughed. I didn't realise, not for a moment—
LIEBERMAN:	And Max … ?
SERGEI:	That was the last time I saw him.
LIEBERMAN:	And ever since his death—
SERGEI:	I've been aware of the presence of Wagner. (PAUSE) Do you like opera, Doctor?
LIEBERMAN:	Would you *like* me to like opera?
SERGEI:	Every question answered with a question.
LIEBERMAN:	Ageing ingénues and overweight Lotharios.
SERGEI:	Is that a yes, or a no?
LIEBERMAN:	No. I do not like opera.

SERGEI:	To me, opera has always been death set to music. Something intoxicatingly ... *lugubrious*. Yet strangely erotic. (PAUSE) Do you have a wife, Doctor Lieberman?

EXT. COVENT GARDEN. DAY.

F/X:	LIEBERMAN AND RUTH PUSH THROUGH THE CROWDS BEHIND THE ROYAL OPERA HOUSE.
RUTH:	All I'm saying, Karl—
LIEBERMAN:	I know what you're saying.
RUTH:	I thought this was supposed to make things easier. 'Move to London', you said. 'We'll spend more time together', you said.
LIEBERMAN:	You see the Pearlmans.
RUTH:	I hate the Pearlmans.
LIEBERMAN:	The Pearlmans hate you. You've got that much in common.
RUTH:	You said we'd see the sights. That is what you said.
LIEBERMAN:	I took you to Freud's house.
RUTH:	Three times.
LIEBERMAN:	There you go. The Royal Opera House. Feast your eyes.

RUTH:	I don't want to see the *building*. I want to see an opera … or the ballet.
LIEBERMAN:	There's just no pleasing you, is there?
RUTH:	Oh … my … *God*.
LIEBERMAN:	What is it? What's wrong?
RUTH:	Look.
LIEBERMAN:	What?
RUTH:	Over there. Isn't that Sergei Bodanov? The conductor?
LIEBERMAN:	I wouldn't know.
RUTH:	Look, it is!
SERGEI:	(OFF) Doctor Lieberman!
RUTH:	You're treating him … Sergei *Bodanov*?
LIEBERMAN:	Just keep walking.
RUTH:	You're treating Sergei Bodanov and you want me to just keep walking?
LIEBERMAN:	Client-therapist confidentiality.
SERGEI:	Doctor Lieberman!
RUTH:	But he's waving at you.
LIEBERMAN:	Please, Ruth.

RUTH:	Ah …
LIEBERMAN:	What? What is it now?
RUTH:	I've twisted my ankle.
LIEBERMAN:	You've done what?
RUTH:	Hereditary. Weak ankles. That's what you get for rushing me.
LIEBERMAN:	That's what I get for marrying you. Can't you just … *limp*?
RUTH:	If you try and make me walk I'll scream the damn place down.
SERGEI:	(OUT OF BREATH) Doctor Lieberman.
LIEBERMAN:	Sergei.
SERGEI:	I was calling.
LIEBERMAN:	I didn't see you.
SERGEI:	I'm so sorry. I didn't mean to interrupt.
LIEBERMAN:	No. You're not interrupting.
RUTH:	(LOW) Well?
LIEBERMAN:	Sergei, sorry, this is my wife, Ruth. Ruth, this is Sergei Bodanov.
SERGEI:	Mrs Lieberman.

RUTH:	Ruth, please. Mrs Lieberman sounds so ... so *old*.
SERGEI:	Ruth.
RUTH:	This is such an honour. I saw *La Traviata* in New York. At the Met.
SERGEI:	You enjoyed it?
RUTH:	Enjoyed it? My God, it was life-affirming.
SERGEI:	I'm so pleased.
RUTH:	I had no idea my husband knew you. You should come to dinner, shouldn't he, Karl?
LIEBERMAN:	(AWKWARDLY) Ruth ... I don't think that Sergei—
RUTH:	Come to dinner. (BEAT) Come to dinner on the weekend.

INT. LAURA'S OFFICE. DAY.

F/X:	LAURA IS ON THE PHONE. DISTANT TRAFFIC OUTSIDE THE OFFICE.
LAURA:	She did what?
LIEBERMAN:	(D) She invited him to dinner.
LAURA:	Couldn't you have stopped her?

LIEBERMAN:	It happened so quickly.
LAURA:	She invited a *client* to dinner?
LIEBERMAN:	Before I knew what had happened, they were exchanging numbers and now she wants to go shopping and get special food … (FADE)

INT. LIEBERMAN'S LOUNGE. NIGHT.

GRAMS:	'NIGHTFALL' BY BENNY CARTER PLAYS QUIETLY ON THE STEREO.
ANSWERPHONE:	You have three messages. Message one.
SERGEI:	(D) Hello, Doctor Lieberman … please, if you're there—
ANSWERPHONE:	Message two.
SERGEI:	Hello? This is Sergei Bodanov, I don't know if you're there—
ANSWERPHONE:	Message three.
SERGEI:	I can't seem to find a pulse. I've been trying for twenty minutes … I've tried both wrists, and nothing … em—
ANSWERPHONE:	End of messages. To delete all messages, press delete.
LIEBERMAN:	You see, Ruth? This is why we do not give out phone numbers to clients.

F/X:	ANSWERPHONE 'BLEEP'.
ANSWERPHONE:	All messages deleted.
RUTH:	So sue me.
LIEBERMAN:	*Sue* you? That's all you can say? Have you got any *idea*—
F/X:	THE PHONE RINGS.
LIEBERMAN:	Oh, God.
RUTH:	Well?
LIEBERMAN:	Don't answer it!
RUTH:	It might be important.
LIEBERMAN:	It won't be. It'll be him.
RUTH:	Who?
LIEBERMAN:	Who? Sergei?
RUTH:	It won't be.
F/X:	RUTH PICKS UP THE PHONE.
RUTH:	Hello?
LIEBERMAN:	I'm not here.
RUTH:	I'll put him on.

LIEBERMAN: Sergei. Hello. Yes … (PAUSE) What sort of headache? *Exactly*?

SCENE SEVEN: INT. LIEBERMAN'S OFFICE. DAY.

SERGEI: When Tchaikovsky conducted, he always kept one hand on his baton, and the other hand on his head. He had a fear, a morbid presentiment that his head would roll off at the podium. Just fall from his neck and drop into the orchestra pit.

LIEBERMAN: But you can see that it was an irrational preoccupation?

SERGEI: Of course. I mean … yes, I could see it was … *should be* irrational. I laughed. Wonderful composer I suppose, if you like your music insipid and Russian. Which, incidentally, I don't. But naturally, the next time I got up to stand at the podium—

LIEBERMAN: You felt a twinge in your neck?

SERGEI: It was a spasm.

LIEBERMAN: I'm sorry?

SERGEI: A shooting pain, right across the larynx and stretching back to the nape of my neck. As if—

LIEBERMAN: As if your neck were suddenly to become bereft of—

SERGEI: My head. As if my neck were suddenly to become bereft of my head.

LIEBERMAN: Ah-ha.

SERGEI: Please don't humour me, Doctor Lieberman. Irrational, I kept telling myself. Completely and utterly irrational. My neck and head arrived at the opera attached and there was no rational hypothesis that would suggest an untimely interruption of the status quo.

LIEBERMAN: Neck and head in perfect harmony.

SERGEI: Exactly.

LIEBERMAN: I see.

SERGEI: But is it that simple?

LIEBERMAN: Perhaps not?

SERGEI: Oh God, you think?

LIEBERMAN: No. No, I meant—

SERGEI: Some ominous undertone of … something … perhaps?

LIEBERMAN: No.

SERGEI: That was a certain, absolute, non-rhetorical, 'no'.

LIEBERMAN:	Was it?
SERGEI:	And back we go to square one. (PAUSE) Do I look well?
LIEBERMAN:	Do you *feel* well?
SERGEI:	I went to the Ivy … yesterday … for lunch. Emile Daeneker was there. My Tristan … the man who told me about Max. He was having lunch with an emaciated cellist. She said I looked well, which either means I look fat or ill. Or both.
LIEBERMAN:	Perhaps she just means that you look … *well*.
SERGEI:	Oh God, as bad as that?
LIEBERMAN:	No, I only meant—
SERGEI:	Emile said I should have a holiday. Assuming *Tristan* ends before I do. 'Go to Lübeck,' he said, 'it'll cheer you up'. Those exact words.
LIEBERMAN:	Why don't you?
SERGEI:	Have you ever been 'cheered up' by a town with an umlaut?
LIEBERMAN:	Ah …
SERGEI:	The air is too cold. The chocolate, artery-clogging. Even the

cuckoo clocks are potentially
life-threatening.

LIEBERMAN: The water's good.

SERGEI: I am deeply suspicious of 'good water'.
              (PAUSE) George Bernard Shaw was a
              friend of Wagner. Did you know that?

LIEBERMAN: George Bernard Shaw was friends with
              everybody. Hitler, Mussolini. You only
              had to be in the same room as George
              Bernard Shaw and he would befriend
              you.

SERGEI: But what a talent. Socially I mean.

LIEBERMAN: It was an obsessive-compulsive
              disorder.

SERGEI: A fellow sufferer. How reassuring.
              (PAUSE) I'm very much looking forward
              to dinner tomorrow, Doctor Lieberman.
              It was so kind of your wife to invite me.

LIEBERMAN: Sergei, I'm sorry. Could we get back
              to—

SERGEI: Yes, of course. To the matter in hand.

LIEBERMAN: Thank you.

SERGEI: (PAUSE) I once bought a self-help video
              on obsessive-compulsive disorder.

LIEBERMAN: Did it help?

SERGEI: I watched it again, and again, and again … (FADE)

INT. LIEBERMAN'S KITCHEN. NIGHT.

F/X: THE KITCHEN IS A HIVE OF PRE-DINNER ACTIVITY. IN THE BACKGROUND, THIRTIES JAZZ PLAYS ON THE STEREO.

RUTH: Pass the pesto, Karl.

LIEBERMAN: Is this the pesto?

RUTH: Does it say pesto on the label?

LIEBERMAN: Yes.

RUTH: Then it's the pesto.

LIEBERMAN: This is why we moved to London. To avoid cranks like Sergei Bodanov.

RUTH: You always tell me off when I call them cranks.

LIEBERMAN: When I call them cranks it's a clinical term.

RUTH: He's just a little sick. That's all.

LIEBERMAN: We're all of us sick, Ruth. Just some are sicker than others.

RUTH: Is that a scientific analysis?

LIEBERMAN: I'm a doctor. Everything I say is
               scientific analysis.

RUTH: So this is a no win situation? Trust you,
               you're a doctor? The pasta's boiling
               over.

LIEBERMAN: Well help me!

RUTH: Drain it … drain it … it's pasta, this is
               not rocket science. Tip it in the bowl.
               No, the blue one … the *blue* one.

LIEBERMAN: The bowl's green. This is a green bowl.
               (PAUSE) Oh God.

RUTH: What?

LIEBERMAN: We shouldn't be doing this. *I* shouldn't
               be doing this.

RUTH: Even patients have to eat.

LIEBERMAN: Client, Ruth. He's a *client*.

RUTH: Whatever.

LIEBERMAN: You know that's not the point. You do
               know that?

RUTH: Fine, I'll eat here, you go eat someplace
               else.

LIEBERMAN: I'm not leaving you on your own with
               him.

RUTH:	Is he dangerous? Psychotic?
LIEBERMAN:	If he was, I'd happily leave you on your own.

F/X: THE DOORBELL RINGS.

RUTH:	Well go on, Karl. Answer the door.
LIEBERMAN:	This is wrong. All wrong. On so many levels.
RUTH:	Door.
LIEBERMAN:	He's my *client*.
RUTH:	Well tonight he's our guest. Do I look okay?
LIEBERMAN:	You've looked worse.
RUTH:	Great. Thanks.

F/X: LIEBERMAN EXITS THE KITCHEN. THE
                FRONT DOOR IS OPENED.

LIEBERMAN:	(OFF) Sergei, good evening … (FADE)

INT. DINING ROOM. NIGHT.

SERGEI:	The food was wonderful, Ruth.
RUTH:	Thank you. More wine, Sergei?
SERGEI:	Perhaps another glass.

RUTH:	Karl?
LIEBERMAN:	No. Thank you.
RUTH:	(READING) Château Cant—
SERGEI:	Château Cantemerle, '96.
RUTH:	You know, I really marvel at people who can distinguish between wines. Not just, 'this is red, that is white'. Connoisseurs.
SERGEI:	What do you do, Ruth?
RUTH:	I'm a lawyer.
SERGEI:	A lawyer?
RUTH:	Matrimonial law.
SERGEI:	That must be very satisfying work.
RUTH:	It can be.
SERGEI:	When I divorced my wife it was the most satisfying thing I'd ever done.
RUTH:	I haven't practised since we left the States.
SERGEI:	How long have you been living in London?
RUTH:	Almost eight months. We moved over last fall.

LIEBERMAN: I studied here, in the Eighties.

RUTH: So what happened? Why did you divorce?

SERGEI: Irreconcilable similarities. I was a neurotic and so was she. She also had an irritating habit of referring to herself in the third person. Sergei did not like this.

RUTH: Karl does a lot of marriage guidance counselling.

SERGEI: I'll bear that in mind if I ever get married again.

LIEBERMAN: Coffee?

RUTH: Later.

SERGEI: How did you both meet? Sorry, that was rude—

RUTH: No. Karl was treating me.

LIEBERMAN: I didn't just take my work home with me, I married it. Her.

RUTH: Panic attacks. Very mild.

SERGEI: But you seem so—

RUTH: Sane?

LIEBERMAN: Sane?

SERGEI: Calm. I was going to say calm.

RUTH: You're very kind.

SERGEI: Very honest.

RUTH: (BEAT) Karl, you can make the coffee now.

INT. LIEBERMAN'S BEDROOM. NIGHT.

F/X: LIEBERMAN CLIMBS INTO BED.

LIEBERMAN: You were all over the man.

RUTH: Flattering, Karl. Very flattering.

LIEBERMAN: I'm surprised you didn't just … copulate … on the table.

RUTH: There was food on the table.

LIEBERMAN: I'm being serious.

RUTH: Sergei was very charming. I just wanted him to have a good evening. I was being a good hostess.

LIEBERMAN: A hooker would have been less accommodating.

RUTH: Thank you for that, honey. (PAUSE) The Pearlmans called today.

LIEBERMAN: Don't change the subject. Good night, Ruth.

RUTH:	We never talk anymore, Karl.
LIEBERMAN:	Ruth, we've never talked. Not together. You talk, I listen.
RUTH:	Like therapy.
LIEBERMAN:	No, with therapy I get to walk away.
RUTH:	Sergei talked to me.
LIEBERMAN:	Sergei had been drinking. He had an excuse.
RUTH:	He invited me to the Opera House. To watch rehearsals.
LIEBERMAN:	Now look here. I said, 'no'. That's it. Over. Nada. No telephone calls. No dinners—
RUTH:	I said I'd love to go.

INT. LIEBERMAN'S OFFICE. DAY.

SERGEI:	I had another dream.
LIEBERMAN:	What happened in the dream?
SERGEI:	I was in an office, much like your office. This office.
LIEBERMAN:	But it wasn't me, was it, sitting in the chair?
SERGEI:	No.

LIEBERMAN: No. It was Wagner.

SERGEI: Yes.

LIEBERMAN: Who else could it have been?

SERGEI: You mean ... you knew?

LIEBERMAN: Yes. It's always Wagner. Every dream is Wagner—

SERGEI: You think I'm mad?

LIEBERMAN: Do *you* think you're mad.

SERGEI: (WRYLY) Is it very difficult to become a psychotherapist?

LIEBERMAN: Rhetoric?

SERGEI: Do you think so?

LIEBERMAN: (PAUSE) Do you often think about death? Your own death?

SERGEI: Sometimes. Naturally.

LIEBERMAN: And sometimes *unnaturally*?

SERGEI: Perhaps.

LIEBERMAN: Your time's very nearly up—

SERGEI: A wonderful bedside manner for treating a hypochondriac, Doctor Lieberman.

LIEBERMAN:	Your *session*.
SERGEI:	Three minutes. We have another three minutes. Is everything all right, Doctor … ?
LIEBERMAN:	How are you feeling, Sergei?
SERGEI:	Feeling?
LIEBERMAN:	Yes. You were concerned that you might have been experiencing a mild … heart attack … when you called last night. Late last night.
SERGEI:	Tragedy averted.
LIEBERMAN:	Right. I think we need to talk.
SERGEI:	That's what we've been doing. For the past hour. That's all we've been doing. *Talking*.
LIEBERMAN:	About your telephone calls—
SERGEI:	My … ?
LIEBERMAN:	I know my wife gave you our telephone number, which in hindsight … she maybe shouldn't have done, but—
SERGEI:	Is there a problem?
LIEBERMAN:	No, not a problem … exactly. It's just … if it's a medical concern …

	a genuine *medical emergency* … it might make sense to speak to your GP.
SERGEI:	I see.
LIEBERMAN:	So we have an … *understanding*?
SERGEI:	Certainly.
LIEBERMAN:	Good.

INT. LIEBERMAN'S LOUNGE. NIGHT.

F/X:	A 'BLEEP' FROM THE ANSWERHONE.
SERGEI:	(D) Doctor Lieberman … it's Sergei Bodanov. I'm sorry to call so late. I know you suggested I shouldn't call … so much … but I wondered … as this is an emergency. I can't seem to feel my left hand.

EXT. HAMPSTEAD HEATH. DAY.

F/X:	TRAFFIC CLOSE BY. A BUSKER PLAYS AT A DISTANCE, GROWING LOUDER AS LIEBERMAN AND LAURA WALK.
LAURA:	You've got to stop this.
LIEBERMAN:	What can I do?
LAURA:	Refer him to another therapist.

LIEBERMAN: But he won't stop calling … and
              calling. I'm going out of my mind.
              Figuratively speaking.

LAURA: That's why you need to refer him.

LIEBERMAN: I know, you're right. As always.

LAURA: So, not quite the draw he promised to
              be?

LIEBERMAN: I honestly thought … the Wagner. If
              only Max Blom hadn't died, now *there*
              was a potential client.

LAURA: Every lunchtime the same. No wonder I
              get acid indigestion.

LIEBERMAN: Hmm?

LAURA: Sandwich?

LIEBERMAN: No, I've eaten.

LAURA: I hate to say I told you so.

LIEBERMAN: But you're going to, right? That's what
              you're going to say?

LAURA: I'll just think it then. You'll never know.
              (PAUSE) Karl?

GRAMS: THE BUSKER, NOW CLOSE BY, PLAYS
              WAGNER'S *FLIGHT OF THE VALKYRIES.*

LIEBERMAN: (SHAKEN) It's Wagner. He's playing Wagner.

INT. OPERA REHEARSAL ROOM. DAY.

F/X: A REHEARSAL PIANIST PLAYS AN EXTRACT FROM 'O SINK HERNIEDER, NACHT DER LIEBE' FROM *TRISTAN UND ISOLDE.*

SERGEI: Good afternoon, everybody.

F/X: THE PIANIST STOPS PLAYING.

Thank you. May I introduce Ruth Lieberman, who'll be sitting in on this afternoon's rehearsal. Ruth, this is Emile Daeneker …

EMILE: Very pleased to meet you.

RUTH: I heard you sing Tristan in '96. I'm a big fan, Mr Daeneker.

EMILE: Thank you.

RUTH: (LOW) Is Misha Leinsdorf here?

SERGEI: Whenever possible we try to rehearse Emile and Misha separately.

EMILE: If I was Tristan and Misha was Isolde, I would have drunk the poison in Act One. Gladly. I don't think I could have made it through to Act Three.

SERGEI: Yes, thank you Emile. If you would just
               sit there, Ruth.

RUTH: Here?

SERGEI: Yep. Wonderful. Christopher,
               metronome please.

F/X: THE SLOW, CONSTANT BEAT OF AN
               ELECTRONIC METRONOME.

               Good. We can start. *'O sink hernieder'*.

GRAMS: THE OPENING BARS OF THE DUET.
               EMILE SINGS. FADE.

               INT. LIEBERMAN'S BEDROOM.
               NIGHT.

RUTH: It was incredible. I goose-fleshed.

LIEBERMAN: (CLEANING TEETH) Maybe you're
               menopausal.

RUTH: Up and down my neck. It was …
               overwhelming. You know he's bilingual
               in four languages?

LIEBERMAN: Who?

RUTH: Sergei. Are you listening?

LIEBERMAN: I'm trying very hard not to, honey.
               Anyway, you can't be bilingual in *four*
               languages.

RUTH:	Please stop calling me honey, it makes my flesh creep. It's intensive cardiovascular exercise, conducting. They have to be supremely fit.
LIEBERMAN:	So he's an athlete now?
RUTH:	You can laugh. You're out of condition.
LIEBERMAN:	I'm not *out* of condition. I've never been *in* condition.
RUTH:	You're dribbling toothpaste.
LIEBERMAN:	I know. I *know*.
RUTH:	You try holding a baton in the air for three hours. Try holding anything up for more than three minutes.
LIEBERMAN:	I heard that. I did *hear* that.
RUTH:	Spit, Karl. You're foaming at the mouth.
F/X:	LIEBERMAN SPITS IN THE SINK.
LIEBERMAN:	Look, you've had your fun. You've flown in the face of psychotherapeutic protocol—
RUTH:	So that's what I'm doing … I'm flying in the face of … yeh, right.
LIEBERMAN:	You're obviously trying to punish me for … for something. For some *perceived* wrong I've done you. For

bringing you to England … for not spending enough time with you … for introducing you to the Pearlmans. *Something.*

RUTH: So this is all about you?

LIEBERMAN: Clearly. It's elementary psychology, Ruth. We were studying this in high school.

RUTH: Okay. So … if I said I was meeting Sergei again tomorrow?

LIEBERMAN: I'd say you were bluffing.

RUTH: And I'd say you were a quack. Don't wait up for me.

<u>INT. REHEARSAL ROOM. DAY.</u>

F/X: <u>EMILE SINGS THE END OF 'LAUSCH, GELIEBTER!' FROM *TRISTAN UND ISOLDE*, ACCOMPANIED BY THE REHEARSAL PIANIST. AS HE FINISHES THERE IS A LOUD RUMBLE OF APPLAUSE FROM THE ASSEMBLED GROUP.</u>

SERGEI: Thank you, Emile. Thank you everybody. I think we'll call it a night. (PAUSE) Ruth, you're crying …

RUTH: It's just so … God, I don't know … so … so moving.

Well, it's the effect we're aiming for.

SERGEI: Well, it's the effect we're aiming for.

EMILE: You enjoyed the rehearsal?

RUTH: Oh, yes. Very much.

EMILE: I hear your husband works miracles, Ruth.

RUTH: He likes to think so.

SERGEI: Emile recommended Karl to me.

EMILE: I come from a long line of Wagnerians. There's mental illness in the blood.

SERGEI: Emile's father was a wonderful singer.

EMILE: Unfortunately, he disagreed with psychotherapy. Like Wagner, he was a strong believer in taking the waters at Marienbad. They're supposed to be very therapeutic.

RUTH: Did they help him?

EMILE: He drowned.

SERGEI: Good. Marvellous. Dinner?

EMILE: Good night, Ruth. Sergei.

SERGEI: Good night.

RUTH: Dinner?

SERGEI: You are hungry?

RUTH: Yes.

SERGEI: Good. Good.

INT. RESTAURANT. NIGHT.

RUTH: I'm sorry. I feel …

SERGEI: Nervous?

RUTH: Yes. I don't know why.

SERGEI: Is it me?

RUTH: No. Yes. I don't know.

SERGEI: I'll take that as a compliment.

RUTH: You're so … *cultured*. For God's sake,
              you're a conductor. You're famous. Of
              course I'm nervous.

SERGEI: Any fool can become a conductor.
              Thankfully, not every fool wants to be.

RUTH: Not just opera. Food, wine, theatre …
              you … you speak Italian.

SERGEI: Would you like to speak Italian?

RUTH: Oh yes. Very much.

SERGEI: It's extremely easy.

RUTH:	Now I know you're just saying that.
SERGEI:	No. *Parlo* …
RUTH:	Look at me. I'm going red. I know, I can just feel—
SERGEI:	*Parlo.*
RUTH:	Parlo.
SERGEI:	… *l'Italiano* …
RUTH:	*Italiano* … I know I'm getting it all wrong.
SERGEI:	No, no. *Parlo l'Italiano Bellamente.*
RUTH:	*Parlo l'Italiano* … Bellamente?
SERGEI:	Bella!
RUTH:	Great. What did I say?
SERGEI:	You told me that you speak Italian beautifully.
RUTH:	You're laughing at me.
SERGEI:	No. You do everything beautifully. Do you speak any languages?
RUTH:	I speak a little French.
SERGEI:	All my languages have been learnt from hotel bedrooms.

RUTH: You're teasing me.

SERGEI: No, I'm serious. I can say 'Fire action'
                   in four different languages. Nothing
                   else. *En caso de Incendio … Verhalten in
                   Brandfall … Consignes en cas d'Incendie
                   … In Caso di Incendio …*

RUTH: Oh my God. That is so …

SERGEI: What?

RUTH: So *sexy.*

SERGEI: What qualities do you look for in a
                   man, Ruth?

RUTH: Availability. (SHE LAUGHS)

SERGEI: I'm available.

RUTH: Well, enjoy me with my clothes on, it's
                   as good as it gets. (SHE LAUGHS) Oh
                   my God, you're not joking are you?

SERGEI: I never joke. Come home with me?

                   <u>INT. LIEBERMAN'S LOUNGE. NIGHT.</u>

GRAMS: <u>'AC-CENT-TCHU-ATE THE POSITIVE'
                   BY JOHNNY GREEN PLAYS ON THE
                   STEREO.</u>

LIEBERMAN: (INTO THE PHONE) She's still not home.

LAURA: (D) Have you tried her mobile?

LIEBERMAN:	It's turned off.
LAURA:	What do you want me to do?
LIEBERMAN:	It's ten to twelve. She's been out with him all day.
LAURA:	Ruth's a big girl, Karl. She can look after herself.
LIEBERMAN:	That's what I'm worried about.

INT. SERGEI'S BEDROOM. NIGHT.

GRAMS:	A CLASSIC RECORDING OF 'MILD UND LEISE WIE ER LACHELT' FROM _TRISTAN UND ISOLDE_ PLAYS QUIETLY ON THE STEREO.
RUTH:	(WALKING) It's a beautiful apartment, Sergei.
SERGEI:	My wife had exquisite taste.
RUTH:	Well, she married you.
SERGEI:	She also divorced me.
RUTH:	I want to know everything about you.
SERGEI:	What do you want to know?
RUTH:	Everything. Your family …
SERGEI:	My relationship with my parents was satisfactory. My father defected from

Russia and married a second-rate flautist. I was conceived in the orchestra pit at the Royal Opera House during a matinee performance of *Der Rosen Kavalier*. It was Spring and the production received appalling notices—

RUTH: You had two children?

SERGEI: Yes.

RUTH: Are you close?

SERGEI: They aren't musical.

RUTH: What are you doing?

SERGEI: I'm unbuttoning your blouse.

RUTH: I can see that.

SERGEI: I will then remove your skirt, your bra and—

RUTH: Panties?

SERGEI: … in that order, and spend the night with you.

RUTH: Okay. I just wondered if … (BEAT) … Okay.

SERGEI: Thank you.

<u>INT. LIEBERMAN'S OFFICE. DAY.</u>

LIEBERMAN:	(IMPATIENT, BUT CONTROLLING IT) And what happens in the dream?
SERGEI:	I'm in a doctor's waiting room. I'm sitting in a chair, waiting. But I'm not alone. I'm aware that there are other people in the room.
LIEBERMAN:	Other people?
SERGEI:	Sylvia Plath arrives with a portable cooker … electric, not gas, which is surprising. Ernest Hemingway is flicking through a well-thumbed copy of *Horse and Hound*, and sucking meditatively on a double-barrelled shotgun. It's clearly a celebrity bash. Sylvia Plath, Ernest Hemingway … and Virginia Woolf staring wistfully at the ornamental pond—
LIEBERMAN:	Ah.
SERGEI:	I dislike it intensely when you do that.
LIEBERMAN:	Do what?
SERGEI:	Say 'ah', like you know something I don't.
LIEBERMAN:	Isn't that what you pay me for?
SERGEI:	I don't pay you to say, 'ah'.
LIEBERMAN:	The dream is sexual. Obviously.

SERGEI:	Uncharacteristically candid, Doctor Lieberman.
LIEBERMAN:	Any impaired sexual activity? Impotence?
SERGEI:	I'm sorry?
LIEBERMAN:	Have you ever used a prostitute?
SERGEI:	For what?
LIEBERMAN:	Look, Sergei …
SERGEI:	Are you all right?
F/X:	<u>LIEBERMAN POURS A GLASS OF</u> <u>WATER.</u>
LIEBERMAN:	Water?
SERGEI:	No, thank you.
LIEBERMAN:	(DRINKS THE WATER) Sergei, there are other forms of therapy you could consider.
SERGEI:	But I don't want other forms of therapy. I want to be cured by *you*.
LIEBERMAN:	Jungian Psychotherapy, maybe, I could recommend somebody good—
SERGEI:	I've read about it. Apparently it isn't necessary to be ill in order to have Jungian Psychotherapy.

LIEBERMAN: No, not necessary. Useful perhaps—

SERGEI: It's useful to be mentally ill?

LIEBERMAN: Only if you're undergoing Jungian Psychotherapy.

SERGEI: But I'm not.

LIEBERMAN: No. Cognitive Therapy?

SERGEI: I don't think so, do you?

LIEBERMAN: Re-birthing?

SERGEI: I'm claustrophobic.

LIEBERMAN: Shock therapy?

SERGEI: I dislike surprises.

LIEBERMAN: Look—

SERGEI: What?

LIEBERMAN: Leave. Please. You're happy.

SERGEI: I'm not.

LIEBERMAN: I've cured you.

SERGEI: No you haven't.

LIEBERMAN: Go.

SERGEI: Should I call for somebody?

INT. LAURA'S OFFICE. DAY.

LAURA: I don't know why you bother coming
           to me. I keep telling you. There are
           other therapists whose brains you
           could pick and spit out.

LIEBERMAN: Laura … we're friends—

LAURA: Why didn't you refer him when I told
           you?

LIEBERMAN: I think he's having an affair with Ruth.

LAURA: (PAUSE) Oh my God.

LIEBERMAN: I don't know what to do.

LAURA: Karl, there's only one thing you can—

LIEBERMAN: I can't refer him. Not now.

LAURA: Listen to yourself. That's …
           completely—

LIEBERMAN: What? Completely what?

LAURA: Unethical. For God's sake—

LIEBERMAN: Nobody else knows, apart from you.

LAURA: You're putting me in a really difficult
           position.

LIEBERMAN: I tried to refer him but he just wouldn't
           go.

LAURA: I told you from the start. 'Avoid hypochondriacs'. Psychotherapist beware. The 'Wagner Complex'. That could have been interesting, something to get your teeth into. Auditory hallucinations, fine. But all you have is a terminal hypochondriac—

LIEBERMAN: Who's sleeping with my wife. (PAUSE) A terminal hypochondriac?

LAURA: You want a cup of coffee?

LIEBERMAN: (TRAVELLING ON LINE) Sorry Laura, I gotta go. I've got a client at three.

LAURA: Phone me. Anytime.

LIEBERMAN: I will. (HE EXITS)

LAURA: I know.

INT. SERGEI'S BEDROOM. NIGHT.

F/X: A RUSTLE OF POST-COITAL ACTIVITY. AN ORGASMIC ARIA FROM *TRISTAN UND ISOLDE* PLAYS ON THE STEREO.

RUTH: Oh my God!

SERGEI: Are you all right?

RUTH: All right? That was *incredible*. Spiritual almost. Wow!

F/X: RUTH ROLLS OVER IN BED.

RUTH: For a hypochondriac, you're very good
          in bed.

SERGEI: What did you tell Karl?

RUTH: I told him that I was spending the
          night at Eva Pearlman's.

SERGEI: Again?

RUTH: Again. (PAUSE) When we're making love
          … you never get the feeling you're
          going to have a heart attack … or
          anything?

SERGEI: Oh God.

RUTH: Sorry. I just thought … you know …
          being a hypochondriac—

SERGEI: Well. You've said it now.

F/X: SERGEI DIALS OUT ON HIS MOBILE
          PHONE.

RUTH: Who are you calling?

SERGEI: Karl.

RUTH: Oh, great. We're in bed together and
          you're phoning my husband for therapy.

SERGEI: There's no answer.

F/X: PAUSE. AT A DISTANCE, SERGEI'S
          LAND LINE RINGS.

RUTH:	Leave it. Stay here.
F/X:	SERGEI GETS OUT OF BED AND PADS ACROSS THE FLOOR.
SERGEI:	It might be Karl.
RUTH:	Sergei!
F/X:	SERGEI PICKS UP THE PHONE.
SERGEI:	Hello. Hello? I know there's somebody there. Who is it?
RUTH:	Sergei?
SERGEI:	They've hung up.
F/X:	SERGEI DIALS 1471.
SERGEI:	It's a withheld number.
RUTH:	(SUGGESTIVELY) I'm getting cold.
	INT. LIEBERMAN'S OFFICE. DAY.
LIEBERMAN:	And this has happened several times?
SERGEI:	The phone rings and there's *nobody there.*
LIEBERMAN:	It happens, Sergei. People dial wrong numbers.
SERGEI:	No. It's not that. It's more than that. It was only once or twice to begin with.

	That was bad enough. But now. My home phone … the mobile … it's always ringing. Blank pages coming through on the fax …
LIEBERMAN:	I see.
SERGEI:	This is exactly what happened to Max. I'm being haunted.
LIEBERMAN:	Haunted?
SERGEI:	You *know*.
LIEBERMAN:	(LOW) Richard Wagner?
SERGEI:	I'm more mad than when we started.
LIEBERMAN:	You weren't mad. You were depressed.
SERGEI:	And *now* I'm mad?
LIEBERMAN:	More depressed.
SERGEI:	Should it work like that? Or am I missing the point here?
LIEBERMAN:	Think of it as a cycle.
SERGEI:	Light at the end of the tunnel?
LIEBERMAN:	Something like that.
SERGEI:	Thank you, Doctor Lieberman … for not referring me. I'm sure … I *know* … only you can help me.

INT. LIEBERMAN'S LOUNGE. NIGHT.

GRAMS:	'HAPPY DAYS ARE HERE AGAIN' BY PAT O'MALLEY PLAYS LOUDLY ON THE STEREO.
RUTH:	I'm moving out for a few days.
LIEBERMAN:	Excuse me? What?
RUTH:	I'm moving out for …
F/X:	RUTH SWITCHES OFF THE STEREO.
	I'm moving out for a few days.
LIEBERMAN:	Goodbye then.
RUTH:	That's all you're going to say? 'Goodbye then'?
LIEBERMAN:	Ciao. Sayonara. What do you want me to say?
RUTH:	Okay. Sergei says—
LIEBERMAN:	Oh, I see. So that's where you're going … *Sergei*. I suppose this was his idea?
RUTH:	You haven't told him.
LIEBERMAN:	Told him what?
RUTH:	That you know about us. (BEAT) Well, have you?

LIEBERMAN:	No. Have you?
RUTH:	No. I'm going to look after him.
LIEBERMAN:	The sick, leading the sick?
RUTH:	You bastard! You cured me.
LIEBERMAN:	Cured you? You're a one-woman psychiatric ward. I could retire and spend the rest of my life treating you. You're a mess.
RUTH:	That's not true.
LIEBERMAN:	And it all stems from low self-esteem.
RUTH:	(LOW) I don't have low self-esteem.
LIEBERMAN:	You're pathetic. Neurotic. Self-loathing—
RUTH:	I'll divorce you! That'll knock a hole through your marriage guidance work. Credibility nil.
LIEBERMAN:	That's perverse.
RUTH:	What is?
LIEBERMAN:	A matrimonial lawyer divorcing a marriage guidance councillor?
RUTH:	It makes perfect sense to me.
LIEBERMAN:	Of course it makes perfect sense to you, you're delusional. You can arrange

the divorce and I'll help us to get over it?

RUTH: For the first time in my life I start having some fun, and all you want to do is ruin it.

LIEBERMAN: Divorce me then, see if I care.

RUTH: Grow up, Karl.

LIEBERMAN: Me grow up? Have you stopped and thought about all of this? If Sergei found out that I know about you two? Who do you think he'd drop first? The menopausal floozy, or the trusted psychotherapist?

RUTH: You're a prick.

LIEBERMAN: You knew that when you married me.

RUTH: You're a real piece of work. You know that?

LIEBERMAN: Of course I know that. I analyse. That's what I do.

RUTH: You've always got to have the last word.

LIEBERMAN: Yes.

RUTH: Goodbye Karl.

LIEBERMAN: (BEAT) Goodbye.

INT. LIEBERMAN'S OFFICE. DAY.

LIEBERMAN: You seem distracted, Sergei?

SERGEI: Distracted?

LIEBERMAN: First preview performance next week?

SERGEI: Yes.

LIEBERMAN: Rehearsals going well?

SERGEI: Rehearsals. Yes. Yes, rehearsals are going well.

LIEBERMAN: But?

SERGEI: I've been feeling rather … ill.

LIEBERMAN: Ah. The hypochondria. Remember, Sergei, a brave man dies only once.

SERGEI: Is that supposed to help?

LIEBERMAN: Did it?

SERGEI: Not at all.

LIEBERMAN: Ah. The point is, Sergei, I can't tell you if you're ill … *physically* ill. I just don't know. How the hell could I know? It's quite possible that you're absolutely fine, but then—

SERGEI: But then?

LIEBERMAN: It's equally possible that you might not be. The human shell can hide a multitude of sins, Sergei. The ache that you feel right down the side of your head … it may be a spasm, who's to say? But … you may be haemorrhaging as we speak. I just don't know from looking at you. There's no way I can tell. This tightness across your chest, psychosomatic maybe—

SERGEI: Likely, you think?

LIEBERMAN: Possible. Don't ask me, ask a doctor.

SERGEI: But you *are* a doctor.

LIEBERMAN: Well, yes, I'm the right doctor to ask if you *think* there's something wrong with you. But if there really *is* something wrong with you. You could be dead on the couch before I count to one … two … (HE CLICKS HIS FINGERS)

SERGEI: So you're telling me there is something wrong? Something seriously wrong with me?

LIEBERMAN: No.

SERGEI: Thank God. For a minute—

LIEBERMAN: You're not listening to what I'm saying, Sergei. You could drop dead next week, at the first preview of *Tristan und Isolde*.

Who can say? We never know our
time's up until it's—

F/X: A BUZZER SOUNDS LOUDLY.

SERGEI: (ALARMED) Oh God!

LIEBERMAN: Thank you, Sergei. That's the end of our
                session.

                INT. LAURA'S KITCHEN. NIGHT.

F/X: COFFEE PERCOLATOR IN ACTION.

LAURA: Karl, you're not being rational.

LIEBERMAN: Rational? I'm being completely rational.
                Icily rational.

LAURA: Because this is beginning to sound like
                a manic episode.

LIEBERMAN: Listen to me—

LAURA: You can't sleep … easily distracted …
                excitable—

LIEBERMAN: Laura—

LAURA: *Hyper*manic maybe. Coffee?

LIEBERMAN: I've been thinking, you know … a
                therapist takes on a client … and the
                therapist, most times, really wants
                to help the client. To cure the client.
                'Cause that's the whole reason a

	therapist becomes a therapist, right? To cure people, to make people better—
LAURA:	You're babbling, Karl.
LIEBERMAN:	I'm quite aware of the fact. Thank you. Where was I?
LAURA:	Making people better?
LIEBERMAN:	Yes. No.
LAURA:	No?
LIEBERMAN:	Sometimes, and I only say *sometimes* … not *all times* … a therapist, for whatever reason, gets to the point where it's not in his best interests for the client to get any better. Actually, quite the reverse.
LAURA:	Karl?
LIEBERMAN:	Say … and I'm clutching at examples here … say the client runs off with the therapist's wife. Awkward situation … I mean, what would you do?
LAURA:	I'd sit down, very calmly. Breathe. Keep breathing.
LIEBERMAN:	Or say … just for another example … your client had a … I don't know … a morbid fixation with Richard Wagner. Would it be so wrong to phone that client—

LAURA:	Karl … I'm not hearing this.
LIEBERMAN:	… and phone that client. And phone, and phone and phone …
LAURA:	(PAUSE) Karl. Karl, are you okay?
F/X:	LIEBERMAN BEGINS TO SNORE.
	Shit.

INT. SERGEI'S APARTMENT. DAY.

F/X:	A SERIES OF ANSWERPHONE 'BLEEPS'.
RUTH:	Sergei, if you're there, please answer the phone. Come on, pick up. It's me, Ruth. I've been trying you all day. I just wanted to wish you luck for tonight … (FADE)

INT. ROYAL OPERA HOUSE. NIGHT.

F/X:	THE ORCHESTRA WARMS UP IN THE PIT. THE HUM OF AUDIENCE CONVERSATION. LIEBERMAN TAKES HIS SEAT.
RUTH:	I didn't think you were going to come.
LIEBERMAN:	And miss Sergei's big night? I think not.
RUTH:	(LOW) Have you been drinking?
LIEBERMAN:	I've had a drink. Yes.

RUTH: Miss me? Drowning your sorrows?

LIEBERMAN: I was celebrating.

F/X: A ROUND OF APPLAUSE AS
                  SERGEI TAKES HIS PLACE AT THE
                  PODIUM.

LIEBERMAN: Well there he is.

RUTH: There he is.

LIEBERMAN: He looks haggard. What are you doing
                  to him?

RUTH: Ssh.

GRAMS: THE ORCHESTRA STRIKES UP WITH
                  THE OVERTURE TO *TRISTAN UND
                  ISOLDE*. FADE.

                  INT. CRUSH BAR. NIGHT.

F/X: THE AUDIENCE SURGES AROUND
                  THE ROOM.

LIEBERMAN: He doesn't look at all well.

RUTH: It sounds like you're gloating.

LIEBERMAN: He's my client, Ruth. I care.

RUTH: Don't, for God's sake, pretend you've
                  got a professional conscience now.
                  That's too hypocritical, even for you.

LIEBERMAN: Do you think he'll survive to the end of
                 the performance?

RUTH: Stop it.

LIEBERMAN: Two Acts down, one to go.

                 INT. ROYAL OPERA HOUSE. NIGHT.

GRAMS: ISOLDE'S CONCLUDING ARIA
                 'MILD UND LEISE WIE ER
                 LACHELT'.

RUTH: My God, it's … it's orgasmic.

LIEBERMAN: You're having an episode. You should
                 have stayed in therapy.

                 INT. ROYAL OPERA HOUSE. NIGHT.

GRAMS: *TRISTAN UND ISOLDE* REACHES ITS
                 CONCLUSION.

RUTH: That was … *wonderful.*

LIEBERMAN: Okay, I suppose. If you like that kind of
                 thing.

F/X: A ROUSING OVATION FROM THE
                 AUDIENCE. SUDDENLY A SCREAM
                 RINGS OUT.

RUTH: What is it? What's wrong?

LIEBERMAN: I don't know. I can't see.

RUTH: Oh my God. Look, Karl. It's Sergei! Oh my God, no.

LIEBERMAN: He's collapsed. (FADE)

INT. HOSPITAL ROOM. NIGHT.

F/X: A CONSTANT 'PING' FROM AN ECG MACHINE.

RUTH: Well?

SERGEI: (PAUSE) I feel absolutely wonderful.

LIEBERMAN: You do?

SERGEI: Apparently *in articulo mortis*, I find all is well.

LIEBERMAN: But the doctor. What did the doctor say?

SERGEI: Well, I've got to stay hooked up to this thing over night, just to be on the safe side.

LIEBERMAN: But—

SERGEI: Panic attack. Nothing more, nothing less. The doctor said I was a perfectly preserved specimen. I think it was intended as a compliment.

RUTH: I was so worried. It's on the front page of the morning papers.

SERGEI:	Ah, good. Free publicity.
LIEBERMAN:	You feel absolutely well?
SERGEI:	Yes, thank you.
LIEBERMAN:	You're sure?
SERGEI:	Cured, I think.
LIEBERMAN:	Cured?
SERGEI:	Of my hypochondria. And Wagner can telephone all he likes.
LIEBERMAN:	Can I have a glass of water?
SERGEI:	Of course. Sparkling or still?
RUTH:	Karl? What's wrong?
LIEBERMAN:	My chest.
RUTH:	(CONCERNED) Karl?
GRAMS:	QUIETLY AT FIRST, GROWING IN VOLUME, THE OVERTURE TO *TRISTAN UND ISOLDE.*
	INT. LAURA'S OFFICE. DAY.
F/X:	THE PHONE RINGS.
LAURA:	(D) You've reached the voice mail of Laura Van Helden. Please leave your

name, number and message after the tone.

F/X: A LONG TONE.

SERGEI: (D) Doctor Van Helden. This is Sergei Bodanov, we met at Doctor Lieberman's funeral. I was one of the Doctor's patients … mild depression and hypochondria … er … I feel so much better now, but … I wake up in the middle of the night, absolutely panic stricken that I'm … I don't know, the spectre of hypochondria … does that make sense? A gnawing, all-consuming terror. What if I become a hypochondriac *again*? I was wondering if I could make an appointment to see you—

ANSWERPHONE: End of messages. To delete all messages press delete.

F/X: ANSWERPHONE 'BLEEP'.

ANSWERPHONE: All messages deleted.

GRAMS: THE MUSIC FADES.

END

After Your Play Has Been Broadcast – A Few Parting Thoughts

Will My Producer Call Me Asking for New Ideas?

The benefits of a long-term relationship with a producer are perhaps self-evident. If your first play has been successful, you should theoretically stand a greater chance of selling your next radio play.

A producer will know what is, and equally importantly, what is *not* being bought in a commissioning round. They are your eyes and ears, your spy on the inside – they will be a sounding board, allowing you to kick ideas around, and advise you when there may be an overlap with work that has been slated for production or is in an early stage of development.

It is important to remember that generally speaking, radio is reactive and not proactive. A producer or commissioning editor will usually wait for you to submit an idea, rather than approaching you with a specific idea or subject in mind.

If you've had a productive relationship with your producer, do suggest meeting up to discuss new ideas. Keep in contact and try not to let the grass grow beneath your feet. Out of sight, unfortunately, often means out of mind.

Always Have an Idea up Your Sleeve

If you come up with an idea for a play, write it down. Add to it when you get a moment. Slowly build up a synopsis that might lead to a firm offer proposal.

In the lead-up to an offers round, it's always a good idea to have several back-up ideas (necessity is the mother of invention after all). I'll normally suggest two or three outlines to my producer before a pitch meeting. Then if the commissioning editor bats the chosen idea out of the court, we've still got another couple of ideas to put forward.

Networking

It can be difficult to network beyond your own producer who, in effect, becomes gatekeeper to the world of radio drama. But the more frequently you write for radio, the more likely it is that you'll be introduced to other producers. There are some producers who guard their writers with near Gollum-like care – but even the most possessive producer will understand that it makes sense for a writer to work with a different producer on occasions. Personally, I think it's good to mix it up a bit every now and then. Apart from anything else, you may find that you come up with an idea that simply isn't your usual producer's cup of tea.

Eyes on the Prize

And what about prizes? There are a number of specific awards for radio plays. These include the Richard Imison award for a first-time radio dramatist, the Tinniswood Award, the BBC Audio Drama awards and the Prix Italia.

It's worth noting that in most cases the decision of the judging panel will be based on the quality of the script, and not the quality of the production.

I recently judged a comedy drama award, and the winning entry dramatised the day in 1982 when Anglesey broke free of the Welsh mainland and set sail, circling the British Isles and returning safely to its former mooring point. Could you achieve this on film? Well, probably. Would it be as good? We could argue the point – but I honestly believe that the 'sight' of Anglesey under full sail will always be richer if played out in the listener's imagination.

Writing Courses

There are many courses on offer to budding dramatists – from brief residential courses to full-time academic courses.

The Arvon Foundation runs week-long residential radio writing courses, which can be an invaluable opportunity to work with established radio producers and radio dramatists. I know many first-time radio writers who have forged relationships with writers and producers on just such a course.

Often, an Arvon course has led to the participants creating a network of support once they return home, keeping in regular contact and even reading and reporting on new plays generated by the group.

Read as Many Plays as You Can

Although radio drama scripts are rarely published these days vintage texts can be found. Some of Tom Stoppard's early radio plays are still in print. *Artist Descending a Staircase* and *The Dog It Was That Died* are masterpieces of the medium and are well worth a read. Many radio scripts are also downloadable on the internet.

And if you can't easily get hold of radio plays, then read stage plays and screenplays. Good dialogue is good dialogue right across the board.

A Community of Radio Writers?

If there is an underground (or even overground) network of radio dramatists I've yet to find it. What I would say is this – if you ever encounter a dramatist who writes for radio and you hit it off, do everything you can to nurture this relationship. Create your own support network!

Fortunately for me, one of my closest playwright friends is also a radio dramatist. It's always hard handing over a play for the first time, but it's infinitely easier to pass a script into the hands of a kindly reader who understands the process that has led to the completion of this first, precious draft.

If you don't happen to have a writer friend, no matter. Any trusted friend can become a sounding board – but try to choose the most objective friend.

Never Dismiss the Impossible

It's always important to challenge yourself as a radio dramatist. Nothing is ever impossible on radio. Even if you think you have come up with an idea that can't be achieved, there will always be a way to make it work.

NEVER ask 'What *can't* I do?'

ALWAYS ask 'What *can* I do?'

Altaban the Magnificent by the former BBC radio-writer-in-residence Sebastian Baczkiewicz was a brilliant example of a play which, theoretically, should never have worked on radio. Set in Germany at the end of the Second World War, the play revolved around a mystical and mute giant. The character didn't communicate a single word in the entire 45-minute play. On paper, it was an idea that simply shouldn't have worked. A mute giant? Seriously? *Mute*? I'd like to have been a fly on the wall at that commissioning meeting. And yet it did work. The play deliberately sets out to challenge the listener – and the listener, flattered to be entrusted with the task of conjuring up a three-dimensional character entirely in their own imagination, plays along.

And this is the magic of radio!